40 DAYS

Prayers *and* Devotions
Reflecting *on the* Cross *of* Christ

Book 5

40 DAYS

Prayers *and* Devotions Reflecting *on the* Cross *of* Christ

DENNIS SMITH

Pacific Press®
PUBLISHING ASSOCIATION

Nampa, Idaho
Oshawa, Ontario, Canada
www.pacificpress.com

Cover design by square1studio
Cover design resources from iStock.com
Inside design by square1studio

The author assumes full responsibility for the accuracy of all facts and quotations as cited in this book.

Unless otherwise noted, all Scripture quotations are from the King James Version.

Scripture quotations marked NIV are from the HOLY BIBLE, NEW INTERNATIONAL VERSION®. Copyright © 1973, 1978, 1984, 2011 by Biblica, Inc.® Used by permission. All rights reserved worldwide.

Texts credited to NKJV are from the New King James Version®. Copyright © 1982 by Thomas Nelson, Inc. Used by permission. All rights reserved.

You can obtain additional copies of this book by calling toll-free 1-800-765-6955 or by visiting http://www.adventistbookcenter.com.

Library of Congress Cataloging-in-Publication Data:

Smith, Dennis Edwin, 1944–
    40 days : prayers and devotions reflecting on the cross of Christ / Dennis Smith.
        pages cm
    ISBN 978-0-8163-5718-5 (pbk.)
    1. Jesus Christ—Crucifixion—Prayers and devotions. I. Title. II. Title: Forty days.
    BT450.S65 2015
    232.96'3—dc23
                            2014048056

February 2017

Contents

Section V: Lessons of the Cross

Let this mind be in you, which was also in Christ Jesus: Who, being in the form of God, thought it not robbery to be equal with God: But made himself of no reputation, and took upon him the form of a servant, and was made in the likeness of men: And being found in fashion as a man, he humbled himself, and became obedient unto death, even the death of the cross.

—Philippians 2:5–8

Introduction

This study and prayer devotional is the fifth in a series. As with the first four, this one is designed to prepare God's church for Christ's second coming and to reach outside the fold to call others to join us in getting ready for that glorious event. The preparation begins with church members who are willing to commit themselves to forty days of prayer and devotional study through which they will develop a closer relationship with Jesus Christ and to pray every day for five individuals whom the Lord has put on their heart.

The devotional studies in this book focus on the cross of Christ. The cross has always been central to Christian faith. What in the world of that day was an instrument of torture and a symbol of shame became instead to Christians a symbol of victory. Paul, the greatest Christian theologian of his generation, called the preaching of the cross "the power of God" (1 Corinthians 1:18), and he stated his desire to glory only in the cross (Galatians 6:14). This devotional is intended to uplift the cross of Christ and to draw all who read it to the One who died there for us. Learning what the cross means and experiencing the lessons it bears for us are essential for all who want to be ready when Christ returns.

If you want to draw nearer to Jesus and to reach out to those whom God has put on your heart who have either once known the truth of God's Word and have slipped away or have never known Christ as their personal Savior, then this forty days of devotional studies and prayer is for you. To help you achieve this, I suggest that you choose five people for whom you will pray during the forty days. They may be family members, friends, coworkers, or just about anyone else. Write their names on the "Daily Prayer List" in appendix A. During the forty days, you are to pray for them every day and to use the "Activities to Show You Care" (appendix B) to determine what the Lord wants you to do to reach out to them. Appendix C is a "Suggested Greeting for Prayer Contact" you can use when you call those on your prayer list to inform them you will be praying for them during the next forty days and ask them what they want you to pray for. These forty days will then bless both you and those for whom you pray.

Prayer's Central Role

Prayer is the most powerful force on earth. It is essential for one's own personal spiritual growth, and it is the most effective means of reaching others for Christ. Concerning prayer and the Christian's spiritual growth, Ellen White wrote: "Prayer is the breath of the soul. It is the secret of spiritual power. No other means of grace can be substituted, and the health of the soul be preserved. Prayer brings the heart into immediate contact with the Well-spring of life, and strengthens the sinew and muscle of the religious experience. Neglect the exercise of prayer, or engage in prayer spasmodically, now and then, as seems convenient, and you lose your hold on God. The spiritual faculties lose their vitality, the religious experience lacks health and vigor" (*Gospel Workers,* p. 254).

She also recognized the necessity of prayer in leading others to Christ: "Through much prayer you must labor for souls, for this is the only method by which you can reach hearts. It is not your work, but the work

of Christ who is by your side, that impresses hearts" (*Evangelism,* p. 342). "The Lord will hear our prayers for the conversion of souls" (*Messages to Young People,* p. 315).

You must also consider prayerfully ways to reach out to those for whom you are praying, for you will not only be praying for them—you will also be working to bring them closer to Christ and His church. God will bless your efforts when you pray for and work for those on your prayer list. And God will not only use you to win others to Christ; He will also draw you closer to Himself.

Ellen White understood this double blessing. She wrote, "As you work to answer your own prayers, you will find that God will reveal Himself unto you. . . . Begin now to reach higher and still higher. Prize the things of heaven above earthly attractions and inducements. . . . Learn how to pray; learn how to bear a clear and intelligent testimony, and God will be glorified in you" (*The Upward Look,* p. 256). "Their persevering prayers will bring souls to the cross. In cooperation with their self-sacrificing efforts Jesus will move upon hearts, working miracles in the conversion of souls" (*Testimonies for the Church,* vol. 7, p. 27).

Each day's devotional ends with a "Prayer Focus." This provides a suggested prayer for the day that is related both to the devotional subject for the day and to those on your prayer list.

God has designed Christian fellowship to help us to obtain victory over temptation and to grow spiritually. We were not created to stand alone. Paul commands us to pray for one another (Ephesians 6:18). John says that God is calling us to fellowship (1 John 1:3), and Christ said He was especially present when two or three believers fellowship together (Matthew 18:20). So I strongly recommend that you choose a fellow Christian with whom you can discuss the devotional each day and pray for one another and for those you are working to bring to Christ. You don't have to choose someone in your vicinity. You can pray via a phone call as well as in person.

In addition to the blessings provided by the support of a fellow believer, we also need the help of the Holy Spirit. After His resurrection, Jesus told His disciples that they were to wait to receive the baptism of the Holy Spirit before they went forth to proclaim the gospel to the world. "And, being assembled together with them, [Jesus] commanded them that they should not depart from Jerusalem, but wait for the promise of the Father, which, saith he, ye have heard of me. For John truly baptized with water; but ye shall be baptized with the Holy Ghost not many days hence. . . . But ye shall receive power, after that the Holy Ghost is come upon you: and ye shall be witnesses unto me both in Jerusalem, and in all Judaea, and in Samaria, and unto the uttermost part of the earth" (Acts 1:4, 5, 8).

Even though the disciples had spent the past three and a half years with Christ and had seen and participated in a ministry of miracles, they were not ready to witness for Him. They were to wait to receive "the power." When they received the baptism of the Holy Spirit, they would be empowered as never before to witness for Christ. "And when the day of Pentecost was fully come, they were all with one accord in one place. And suddenly there came a sound from heaven as of a rushing mighty wind, and it filled all the house where they were sitting. And there appeared unto them cloven tongues like as of fire, and it sat upon each of them. And they were all filled with the Holy Ghost, and began to speak with other tongues, as the Spirit gave them utterance" (Acts 2:1–4).

Because the baptism of the Holy Spirit, also called the infilling of the Spirit, is so vital to our personal spiritual growth and our witness to others, I strongly suggest that every day during the Prayer Focus, you ask God to fill you with the Holy Spirit.

Benefits of Participating in the 40 Days

By choosing to participate in the forty days of study and prayer, you are entering into an amazing and blessed adventure with the Lord. You will experience a deeper relationship with Him, and you will see the Lord use you to draw others closer to Himself in preparation for His soon return. As you fellowship with your prayer partner and the others participating in the forty days of prayer and devotional study, you will experience a deeper Christian love and unity with your fellow believers, which will also play an important role

in your own spiritual growth.

I recommend that in order to get the most from the forty days of study and prayer, you do it in the morning. That may mean you have to get up a little earlier than usual, but the effort will be well rewarded. If you ask the Lord to wake you so you can have some quality time with Him, He will hear and answer your prayer.

Concerning Christ's devotional life, Ellen White wrote: "Daily He received a fresh baptism of the Holy Spirit. In the early hours of the new day the Lord awakened Him from His slumbers, and His soul and His lips were anointed with grace, that He might impart to others. His words were given Him fresh from the heavenly courts, words that He might speak in season to the weary and oppressed" (*Christ's Object Lessons*, p. 139).

Christ will do the same for you if you ask Him. He very much desires to anoint you with His Spirit in preparation for each new day. This forty-day devotional study is designed to facilitate just that: a daily anointing of God's Spirit for personal spiritual growth and witnessing for Christ.

If you are using this devotional study in preparation for a visitors' Sabbath and/or evangelistic meetings at the end of the forty days, you should add those programs to the "Prayer Focus" each of the forty days.

You can download the *40 Days Instruction Manual* from the Web site at www.40daysdevotional.com at no charge. This manual provides the instruction you need to facilitate a forty-day program in a church or other group setting. Many churches are using this devotional book in this manner, and it is proving to be an effective preparation for evangelistic meetings and for visitors' Sabbaths.

Note

This introduction, the appendixes, and the forty-day devotional studies follow the same format used in the four 40 Days devotionals published by the Review and Herald® Publishing Association.

The 40 Days devotionals are also designed to complement the "Light America Mission"—a program aimed at encouraging personal spiritual growth through study of God's Word, prayer, training, and the sharing of the messages of Revelation 14's three angels.

Begin now to reach higher and still higher. Prize the things of heaven above earthly attractions and inducements. . . . Learn how to pray; learn how to bear a clear and intelligent testimony, and God will be glorified in you.

—The Upward Look, *p. 256*

Why the Cross Was Necessary

Dominion Lost and the Cross

We are told that when God created Adam, He gave him "dominion" in this world: "And God said, Let us make man in our image, after our likeness: and let them have dominion over the fish of the sea, and over the fowl of the air, and over the cattle, and over all the earth, and over every creeping thing that creepeth upon the earth" (Genesis 1:26). The Hebrew word translated "dominion" is *radah,* which means to rule with the authority of a king ruling over his kingdom. The *dominion* or *authority* God gave to Adam was so complete that Adam could give it away—and that is exactly what happened. When Adam chose to reject God's command and yielded to Satan's temptation, he came under Satan's power, and from that point onward Satan had dominion over this world.

This is why when Satan tempted Christ in the wilderness, he said he could give the kingdoms of the world to Christ, because they had been "delivered" to him. Scripture says, "The devil, taking him up into an high mountain, [showed] unto him all the kingdoms of the world in a moment of time. And the devil said unto him, All this power will I give thee, and the glory of them: for that is delivered unto me; and to whomsoever I will I give it. If thou therefore wilt worship me, all shall be thine" (Luke 4:5–7).

One major reason Christ endured crucifixion was to return control of this world to humanity and God. Dominion over this world was given to a man and lost by that same man—Adam. But another Man, Jesus Christ, regained humanity's dominion over this world. "(If by one man's offence death reigned by one; much more they which receive abundance of grace and of the gift of righteousness shall reign in life by one, Jesus Christ.) . . . For as by one man's disobedience many were made sinners, so by the obedience of one shall many be made righteous" (Romans 5:17, 19).

We see this point being made in Revelation 5. There God the Father is depicted as holding a scroll representing the deed to this world, which no one was found worthy to take from the Father. As a result, there was much weeping. Then we read:

One of the elders saith unto me, Weep not: behold, the Lion of the tribe of Judah, the Root of David, hath prevailed to open the book, and to loose the seven seals thereof. And I beheld, and, lo, in the midst of the throne and of the four beasts, and in the midst of the elders, stood a Lamb as it had been slain, having seven horns and seven eyes, which are the seven Spirits of God sent forth into all the earth. And he came and took the book out of the right hand of him that sat upon the throne. And when he had taken the book, the four beasts and four and twenty elders fell down before the Lamb, having every one of them harps, and golden vials full of odours, which are the prayers of saints. And they sung a new song, saying, Thou art worthy to take the book, and to open the seals thereof: for thou wast slain, and hast redeemed us to God by thy blood out of every kindred, and tongue, and people, and nation; And hast made us unto our God kings and priests: and we shall reign on the earth (Revelation 5:5–10).

What follows in that chapter is a crescendo of praise to the Lamb.

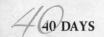

Before the cross of Christ, all humanity was lost. After Christ's victory on the cross, all who believe in Him are redeemed from Satan's dominion and saved in God's kingdom. "[The Father] . . . hath delivered us from the power of darkness, and hath translated us into the kingdom of his dear Son: In whom we have redemption through his blood, even the forgiveness of sins" (Colossians 1:13, 14).

The cross of Christ was no afterthought following Adam's sin. No, the cross of Christ was planned from eternity before the creation of this world. Revelation refers to Christ as "the Lamb slain from the foundation of the world" (Revelation 13:8). As soon as Adam and Eve sinned, there was a Savior. God even foretold what would be done to secure their redemption. In the Garden of Eden, He told the serpent (Satan), "I will put enmity between thee and the woman, and between thy seed and her seed; it shall bruise thy head, and thou shalt bruise his heel" (Genesis 3:15). In other words, God told Satan that he would be destroyed (his head would be bruised). However, in bruising the head of the serpent, the "seed of the woman" (Christ) would be wounded too. This bruising of His heel referred to the cross.

God foresaw all things from eternity. He loved us so much that He chose to create us despite knowing the tragedies sin would bring and what saving us from our sin would cost Him. We should never doubt God's love for us nor His desire and ability to save us. Scripture says, "He is able also to save them to the uttermost that come unto God by him" (Hebrews 7:25).

Discussion Questions

1. **What did God's giving Adam dominion over this earth mean?** _____

_____

2. **What did Satan gain when Adam and Eve yielded to his temptation?** _____

_____

3. **How did heaven react to humanity's fall into sin?** _____

_____

4. **In what ways did Christ's victory on the cross affect Satan's dominion over this world?** _____

_____

5. **Whose kingdom are we in when we accept Jesus Christ as our Savior?** _____

_____

6. **When did God devise the plan of salvation?** _____

_____

7. **What does God's having a plan to save us tell us about His attitude toward us?** _____

_____

Prayer Focus

Pray for:

- **God to fill you with the Holy Spirit.**
- **God to open your understanding of His love for you.**
- **Those on your prayer list.**

Day 2

The Cross and God's Love—Part 1

The Bible tells us that God is love (see 1 John 4:8). It's one thing to say "I love you," but it is quite a different thing to demonstrate that love. People can say the words "I love you" and mean nothing at all by those words. It's sad to say, but many times that is the case with humankind. Many people say those words frequently while simultaneously contradicting them by the way they treat the one's they say they love.

Another complication arises in that the word *love* has many shades of meaning; some deep and some very shallow. It's obvious that the Greeks understood that there were different kinds of love because they had names for three of them: *philia, eros,* and *agapē.**

The Greek word *philia* refers to a brotherly love—a warm-feeling, relational kind of love. *Eros* designates the kind of love that is sensuous and very conditional. This is the kind of love people are referring to when they say, "I love strawberries." If strawberries began to taste like spinach, they would stop "loving" them!

The third Greek word for love is *agapē.* This is the kind of love that gives of itself for the good of the one who is the object of this love. People who love someone with this kind of love do what's good for the one they love rather than what's good for themselves. And *agapē* love is not conditioned on how the ones being loved respond to the love bestowed on them.

Agapē love is the kind of love God has. He loves all humanity; even His enemies. This is why when Christ instructed His disciples to be like their heavenly Father, He told them,

Love your enemies, bless them that curse you, do good to them that hate you, and pray for them which despitefully use you, and persecute you; that ye may be the children of your Father which is in heaven: for he maketh his sun to rise on the evil and on the good, and sendeth rain on the just and on the unjust. For if ye love them which love you, what reward have ye? do not even the publicans the same? And if ye salute your brethren only, what do ye more than others? do not even the publicans so? Be ye therefore perfect, even as your Father which is in heaven is perfect (Matthew 5:44–48).

The cross of Christ reveals God's agape love for each of us. He planned the Cross to save us before we needed saving. He provided the Cross after we sinned, while we were living lives out of harmony with His will. But "God commendeth his love toward us, in that, while we were yet sinners, Christ died for us" (Romans 5:8). God loved us in our most unlovable, sinful condition. Christ demonstrated this kind of love while He hung on the cross. When His enemies were mocking Him, He prayed, "Father, forgive them; for they know not what they do" (Luke 23:34).

All of us are sinners, so all of us deserve to die—"for the wages of sin is death" (Romans 6:23). This sinful world deserves destruction and will finally be destroyed. "The day of the Lord will come as a thief in the night; in the which the heavens shall pass away with a great noise, and the elements shall melt with fervent heat, the earth also and the works that are therein shall be burned up" (2 Peter 3:10). But the fact is that we are able to breathe, and that there is air for us to

---

* The three words are given here in their noun form; *philia* is probably better known in it's verb form *phileō.*

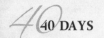

breathe, and that God has supplied this need not in a mere utilitarian way, but in the beauties of clear blue skies and majestic clouds and sunrises and sunsets. All this is a revelation of God's love. We are alive and able to breathe and have the air to breathe and have it in beautiful scenes only because of the cross of Christ. It is because of God's love for us that this sinful world still exists in an otherwise sinless universe. "For God so loved the world, that he gave his only begotten Son, that whosoever believeth in him should not perish, but have everlasting life" (John 3:16).

The cross of Christ is the greatest revelation of love that ever has been and that ever will be exhibited in this universe. It reveals a love that led our Creator to step down from His throne in heaven, become one of us, and die for our sins, for which He had no responsibility. "Let this mind be in you, which was also in Christ Jesus: Who, being in the form of God, thought it not robbery to be equal with God: But made himself of no reputation, and took upon him the form of a servant, and was made in the likeness of men: And being found in fashion as a man, he humbled himself, and became obedient unto death, even the death of the cross" (Philippians 2:5–8).

Amazing love! Amazing grace!

Discussion Questions

1. **What are the three Greek words translated "love" in the Bible, and what does each of these words mean?** _____

   _____

2. **Which word for love is used to describe God?** _____

   _____

3. **What instruction did Jesus give His disciples about how they were to love their enemies?** ___

   _____

4. **How did Jesus demonstrate *agapē* love for His enemies as He hung on the cross?** _____

   _____

5. **List some everyday examples of God's love for us.** _____

   _____

6. **What is the greatest revelation of God's love?** _____

   _____

Prayer Focus

Pray for:

- **God to fill you with the Holy Spirit.**
- **God to reveal to you His love for you.**
- **Those on your prayer list.**

The Cross and God's Love—Part 2

The Cross is the greatest revelation of love that has ever been exhibited in this universe. It is a revelation that the pure, holy, sinless God of the universe chose to step down from His throne and become one of us in order to save a fallen race from the consequences of their disobedience to God. Paul lays out for us in detail what this meant, saying that Christ Jesus, who was "in the form of God, thought it not robbery to be equal with God: But made himself of no reputation, and took upon him the form of a servant, and was made in the likeness of men: And being found in fashion as a man, he humbled himself, and became obedient unto death, even the death of the cross" (Philippians 2:6–8). The cross of Christ is the greatest exhibition of love that has ever been given.

One of the greatest tragedies in this world is that people don't know how much their Creator God loves them. I also believe that many Christians don't really know deep in their hearts how much God loves them either. If someone asked, "Does God love you?" most of us would answer Yes. And if we were asked, "How do you know God loves you?" we would answer, "Jesus came to this world and suffered and died for us."

It's true that God loves us and that Jesus suffered and died for us. But our knowledge of these facts isn't necessarily evidence that we know deep in our hearts that God truly loves us as individuals. We can have a head knowledge of God's love for us without having a heart knowledge of His love.

Paul understood this, which is the reason he prayed for the Ephesian Christians that God would grant them, according to the riches of His glory, to be strengthened with might by His Spirit in the inner man; that Christ might dwell in their hearts by faith; that they, being rooted and grounded in love, might be able to comprehend with all saints what is the breadth, and length, and depth, and height; and to know the love of Christ, which passeth knowledge, that they might be filled with all the fullness of God (see Ephesians 3:16–19).

Paul prayed that the Ephesian Christians would know Christ's love for them on a deep level—one that "passeth knowledge." He prayed that they would know in their hearts that Christ loved them. And then Paul connects this deep knowing of God's love with being filled with the "fullness of God." The deeper in our hearts that we know God loves us, the more of God we will experience.

It is apparent that John understood this, because he wrote, "There is no fear in love; but perfect love casteth out fear: because fear hath torment. He that feareth is not made perfect in love" (1 John 4:18). The deeper the conviction we have in our hearts that God loves us, the less we will doubt and fear. This is why Paul lists love as the first fruit of the Spirit: "The fruit of the Spirit is *love,* joy, peace, longsuffering, gentleness, goodness, faith, meekness, temperance: against such there is no law" (Galatians 5:22, 23; emphasis added). The stronger our conviction that God loves us, the more joy, peace, faith, and so forth we will have.

John pointed out two more essential truths related to our knowing God's love for us. First, he wrote, "We love him, because he first loved us" (1 John 4:19). God takes the initiative. It isn't our love for God that makes Him love us. It is His love for us that creates our love for Him.

Second, John also wrote that "he who loveth God [will] love his brother also" (verse 21). In other words, here John tells us that when we experience God's love for us, we will not only love Him in return, but we will also love those whom He loves.

These points have two important implications. First, how much we love God and other people depends on how much we know of God's love for us. The more of God's love we see, the more we will love Him and other people. And second, as Jesus put it, "If ye love me, keep my commandments" (John 14:15). Again, the truth is that we can obey God's commandments from the heart only if we know deep in our heart that God loves us.

Scripture is clear: knowing deep in our heart that God loves us is foundational to our being able to love God and other people and to obeying God from the heart. If our knowledge of God's love for us is only intellectual, a head knowledge and not a heart knowledge, then our love for God and our obedience to His commandments will be merely intellectual and not from the heart. The more we understand the love of God as revealed in the cross of Christ, the more we will love God and one another, and the more we will become like Jesus Christ in heart and character.

Discussion Questions

1. What is the greatest revelation of God's love? _____

_____

2. What did Paul pray that the the Ephesian Christians would learn—that they would know?

_____

3. What effect will knowing God loves us have on our joy, peace, faith, and so on? _____

_____

4. Write in your own words what John meant when he wrote, "We love him, because he first loved us" (1 John 4:19). _____

_____

5. Write in your own words what John meant when he wrote, "He who loveth God love his brother also" (1 John 4:21). _____

_____

6. What must we know about God in order to truly keep His commandments from the heart?

_____

Prayer Focus

Pray for:

- God to fill you with His Spirit today.
- God to open your understanding of the Cross so that you can know deep in your heart that God loves you.
- The people on your prayer list.

Day 4

The Cross and Man's Relationship With God

When God made man, He made him in His image and likeness: "God said, Let us make man in our image, after our likeness: and let them have dominion over the fish of the sea, and over the fowl of the air, and over the cattle, and over all the earth, and over every creeping thing that creepeth upon the earth. So God created man in his own image, in the image of God created he him; male and female created he them" (Genesis 1:26, 27). The words translated "image" and "likeness" here are the words that are used for what people did when they made an idol. They made the idol in the "image" or "likeness" of their god. So, we learn from these verses of Scripture that humans were created to be very much like their Creator. Humans were made as much like God as a created being could be.

God is a relational being. In fact, the word *Elohim,* which is translated "God," is a plural noun. This tells us that God is a "plural" being. This concept is developed throughout the Bible, but it is most clearly delineated in the New Testament. It means that even before any beings other than God existed, God was a relational being. Father, Son, and Holy Spirit dwelt and worked in very close relationship. Thus when God created man, He meant him to have—He created him to have—an eternal, close relationship with God. We see this illustrated in the Garden of Eden. There God communicated directly with Adam and Eve when He gave them instructions and also when they sinned. Adam and Eve heard the "voice" of God when He was "walking in the garden" (see Genesis 3:8). This implies that they knew God's voice and were used to what was apparently His practice of walking in the garden and talking with them.

Man was a special creation. He was created to be in a unique relationship with God. Satan had some concept of this, and he determined to take man away from God, to sever his relationship with God, and lead him to become very much like himself—an enemy of God.

Paul wrote, "The carnal mind is enmity against God: for it is not subject to the law of God, neither indeed can be. So then they that are in the flesh cannot please God" (Romans 8:7, 8). In these verses the "carnal mind" and being in the "flesh" refer to man's natural-born sinful condition since the fall of Adam and Eve; that is, a condition of not desiring God or being in any meaningful relationship with Him.

Therefore, we learn from Scripture that when Adam and Even sinned, the close, intimate relationship with God that they'd had previously was severed. However, God said in His heart, "I love you so much that I refuse to let you go." Our relationship with God meant so much to Him that He was willing to do whatever was necessary to bring us back into relationship with Him. God indicated this when, soon after humanity yielded to Satan's temptation, He told Satan, "I will put enmity between thee and the woman, and between thy seed and her seed; it shall bruise thy head, and thou shalt bruise his heel" (Genesis 3:15).

We learn several important things from what God told Satan. When Adam and Eve were created, they were in total harmony with their Creator, having been made in His image and likeness. However, after they sinned, they and their children became enemies of God, in harmony with Satan rather than with God.

But God told Adam and Eve and Satan that He was going to change that and bring them back into harmony

19

with Himself. God also said that both He and Satan would pay a price for Adam's sin. Satan's "head" would be "bruised"—meaning that he would receive a mortal wound and ultimately be destroyed. God also would receive a wound in the process of returning human beings to a meaningful relationship with Himself. In the process, the heel of the "seed" of the woman—which refers to Christ, who was born of a woman—would be bruised. This "bruising" of Christ refers to His crucifixion. God in the person of Jesus Christ would pay the price for our sins and for all the sins of all those who accept Christ's sacrifice in their behalf—and thus humankind would be restored to an eternal relationship with God.

This is why being "with" God is a primary purpose of our salvation. Jesus indicated this when He said to the thief on the cross, "you will be with Me in Paradise" (Luke 23:43, NKJV). Paul also emphasizes the fact that the redeemed will "ever be with the Lord" (1 Thessalonians 4:17) when Jesus returns to earth to take them back to heaven with Him (see John 14:1–3). Because of the cross of Christ we can be restored to the eternal, close, meaningful relationship with God that from our creation He intended us to have with Him.

Discussion Questions

1. How does the Bible describe the creation of humankind in relation to God? _____
_____

2. What does God's creation of humankind in God's image and likeness mean? _____
_____

3. Why did God create human beings? _____
_____

4. How did Adam's sin affect the relationship of human beings with God? _____
_____

5. What did God promise to do for fallen human beings, and why did He make that promise?
_____

6. What would happen to Satan and to Christ, "the seed of the woman," when this promise was fulfilled? _____
_____

7. What did Adam and Eve lose that will be restored as a result of the cross of Christ? _____
_____

Prayer Focus

Pray for:

- God to fill you with the Holy Spirit.
- God to open your understanding to how important you are to Him.
- Those on your prayer list.

Day 5

The Cross and Satan's Defeat

When God created Lucifer (see Isaiah 14:12), later known as Satan, he was a very beautiful and wise angel. Referring to Lucifer through the imagery of the king of Tyre, God said, "Son of man, take up a lamentation upon the king of Tyrus, and say unto him, Thus saith the Lord GOD; Thou sealest up the sum, full of wisdom, and perfect in beauty. Thou hast been in Eden the garden of God; every precious stone was thy covering, the sardius, topaz, and the diamond, the beryl, the onyx, and the jasper, the sapphire, the emerald, and the carbuncle, and gold: the workmanship of thy tabrets and of thy pipes was prepared in thee in the day that thou wast created. Thou art the anointed cherub that covereth; and I have set thee so: thou wast upon the holy mountain of God; thou hast walked up and down in the midst of the stones of fire. Thou wast perfect in thy ways from the day that thou wast created, till iniquity was found in thee" (Ezekiel 28:12–15). Lucifer is called the "anointed cherub." That means he was the angel closest to God—in effect, the chief angel.

The word translated "Lucifer" (Isaiah 14:12) means "morning star" or "shining one." Concerning Lucifer, Ellen White wrote: "Was not Satan the lightbearer, the sharer of God's glory in heaven, and next to Jesus in power and majesty?" (*Christian Education,* p. 72). Lucifer, then, had full access to God and all the angels of heaven. However, sad to say, his high position led him to become prideful and ambitious for a higher position than God had created him to fill. Isaiah wrote of this: "How art thou fallen from heaven, O Lucifer, son of the morning! how art thou cut down to the ground, which didst weaken the nations! For thou hast said in thine heart, I will ascend into heaven, I will exalt my throne above the stars of God: I will sit also upon the mount of the congregation, in the sides of the north: I will ascend above the heights of the clouds; I will be like the most High" (Isaiah 14:12–14). Lucifer wanted to be like God; he wanted to be worshiped by the angels.

Lucifer's selfish ambition stirred up a great conflict in heaven between himself and Christ: "There was war in heaven: Michael and his angels fought against the dragon; and the dragon fought and his angels, and prevailed not; neither was their place found any more in heaven" (Revelation 12:7, 8). In this conflict Lucifer convinced a third of the angels to follow him (see verse 4), but his attempt to overthrow God failed. However, as we have seen in a previous day's devotional, he was successful in overthrowing Adam, and thus gained dominion over this world. Hence, Satan became the ruler and representative of planet earth. We see this when we read the portrayal in the book of Job of a meeting of representatives from God's creation that Satan attended. "Now there was a day when the sons of God came to present themselves before the LORD, and Satan came also among them. And the LORD said unto Satan, Whence comest thou? Then Satan answered the LORD, and said, From going to and fro in the earth, and from walking up and down in it" (Job 1:6, 7). From this scripture we learn that Lucifer (Satan) had access to heaven after his efforts to usurp God's position there and even after Adam's fall into sin.

However, the cross of Christ changed this completely. Following the description of the war in heaven between Christ and His angels and Satan and his angels, we read,

The great dragon was cast out, that old serpent, called the Devil, and Satan, which deceiveth the whole world: he was cast out into the earth, and his angels were cast out with him. And I heard a loud voice saying in heaven, Now is come salvation, and strength, and the kingdom of our God, and the power of his Christ: for the accuser of our brethren is cast down, which accused them before our God day and night. . . . Therefore rejoice, ye heavens, and ye that dwell in them. Woe to the inhabiters of the earth and of the sea! for the devil is come down unto you, having great wrath, because he knoweth that he hath but a short time (Revelation 12:9, 10, 12).

The line "Now is come salvation, and strength, and the kingdom of our God, and the power of his Christ" refers to the victory of Christ on the cross. After the crucifixion, Satan no longer had access to heaven; he was "cast down" and limited to planet earth. The events Satan instigated that led to the cross clearly revealed how truly evil and hateful he was toward God.

As a result of the crucifixion, Christ, the second Adam, regained full dominion of the earth and became man's representative before God. Because of the Cross, Satan lost the position and the dominion he had gained through Adam's fall. Now Satan's defeat is sure and his days are numbered. You need not fear this archenemy because in Christ you have authority over him, which is why Christ declared, "Behold, I give unto you power to tread on serpents and scorpions, and over all the power of the enemy: and nothing shall by any means hurt you" (Luke 10:19). Praise God!

Discussion Questions

1. **What kind of angel was Lucifer before his fall into sin, and what led to his fall?** _____
   _____

2. **What did Satan become in relation to planet earth as a result of Adam's yielding to his temptation?** _____
   _____

3. **What effect did the cross of Christ have on Satan's access to heaven?** _____
   _____

4. **Why don't you have to fear Satan?** _____
   _____

5. **Because of the cross of Christ, Satan's fate is assured. What is it?** _____
   _____

Prayer Focus

Pray for:

- **God to fill you with His Spirit.**
- **God to help you better understand the authority you have over Satan because of the Cross.**
- **Those on your prayer list.**

Day 6

The Cross and the Wisdom of God

As we studied in yesterday's devotional, when Lucifer allowed pride and selfish ambition to fill his heart, he began laying plans to "be like the most High" (Isaiah 14:14). This led to a great conflict in heaven that resulted in his being cast out of heaven and down to this earth (see Revelation 12:7–9). However, he was so deceptive in his efforts to overthrow God that one third of the angels chose to follow him (see verse 4).

God could have destroyed Satan and his host of evil angels. However, God knew that for the universe to be eternally secure, He had to allow Satan to continue carrying out his plans so everyone could see that Satan is truly evil and destructive. The higher orders of created beings in the universe are intelligent, and they were tempted to listen to Satan's charges against God. It's important that all questions about God's righteousness, fairness, and love be clearly answered and even proved.

This explains why God has chosen to allow the conflict between Himself and Satan to be carried out in this world. That's what Paul had in mind when he wrote that the apostles were "made a spectacle unto the world, and to angels, and to men" (1 Corinthians 4:9). The Greek word translated "spectacle" means a theater where drama is performed and a place where people meet to hear debates. The great drama between God and Satan is being played out here on planet earth for all to see. In the end God will be proved just, righteous, and loving, and "at the name of Jesus every knee should bow, of things in heaven, and things in earth, and things under the earth; and that every tongue should confess that Jesus Christ is Lord, to the glory of God the Father" (Philippians 2:10, 11). Sin, Satan,

and his evil host will come to an end, and sin will never arise again because all will know that God is a loving father.

Without the cross of Christ, God would not be vindicated, because it is the Cross that has made the greatest revelation of God's love ever seen: "In this was manifested the love of God toward us, because that God sent his only begotten Son into the world, that we might live through him. Herein is love, not that we loved God, but that he loved us, and sent his Son to be the propitiation for our sins" (1 John 4:9, 10).

God's plan to save humanity from sin reaches two very important goals. First, God is revealed and vindicated as a loving God. Second, salvation is provided for those human beings who accept Christ as their Savior. God's plan to save humanity is called the "wisdom" of God. The revealing of God's "wisdom" was accomplished through Jesus Christ. "His intent was that now, through the church, the manifold wisdom of God should be made known to the rulers and authorities in the heavenly realms, according to his eternal purpose that he accomplished in Christ Jesus our Lord" (Ephesians 3:10, 11, NIV).

It is important to note that according to Paul, before Jesus returns, the "wisdom of God" must be made known or manifest in His church (His people). This "wisdom of God" was "accomplished in Christ," and it is to be revealed through the church so "rulers and authorities in the heavenly realms" will see it. This is the church's primary purpose or mission on earth.

Here's a vital question: What is the wisdom of God that was accomplished in Christ? Paul gives the answer in his first letter to the Corinthians. He tells us that God

23

works through the foolish, and the weak, and the poor "so that no one may boast before him. It is because of him that you are in Christ Jesus, who has become for us wisdom from God—that is, our righteousness, holiness [sanctification], and redemption. Therefore, as it is written: 'Let the one who boasts boast in the Lord' " (1 Corinthians 1:29–31, NIV).

You see, the wisdom of God is the righteousness, sanctification (holiness), and redemption that Christ provided for His people. This wisdom of God will be made known to the rulers and authorities in the heavenly realms as the church (you and I) experiences having Christ in our lives to the fullest extent. It is

His righteous life, death on the cross, and resurrection that made it possible for humans to become righteous through Christ's righteousness, sanctified by Christ living out His righteousness in them, and redeemed from the guilt and penalty of sin in order to receive eternal life, thus truly revealing the "wisdom" of God. This is why God has called you to accept Christ as your personal Savior. He has called you to be righteous, sanctified, and redeemed through Jesus Christ; to make known the wisdom of God "to the rulers and authorities in the heavenly realms."

Discussion Questions

1. **How many of the angels believed Lucifer's lies about God and chose to follow him?** _____

   _____

2. **Why didn't God destroy Lucifer and the evil angels soon after they sinned?** _____

   _____

3. **What does the cross of Christ reveal about the kind of being God is?** _____

   _____

4. **What is the "wisdom" of God?** _____

   _____

5. **How can you reveal the wisdom of God in your life?** _____

   _____

6. **What part do you have in vindicating God before the universe?** _____

   _____

Prayer Focus

Pray for:

- **God to fill you with the Holy Spirit.**
- **God to lead you to experience Christ's righteousness, sanctification, and redemption.**
- **Those on your prayer list.**

Day 7

The Cross and the Holy Spirit

In a previous devotional we saw that when Adam yielded to Satan's temptation in the Garden of Eden, he lost the dominion over this world that God had given him. Tragically, this enabled Satan to take dominion over the earth. That, in turn, affected the extent to which the Holy Spirit could influence even God's people. This is why in the Old Testament we find that only a few individuals—for example, Moses and the prophets— were filled with the Spirit when God called them to do a unique work for Him.

Because of Adam's fall and Satan's taking for himself the dominion over this earth that God had given Adam, God became somewhat limited. If God didn't wrest that dominion over planet earth and its inhabitants from Satan, the earth and all that is in it would have had to be destroyed. Planet earth would be eternally lost.

This explains the great rejoicing Revelation 5 pictures when Christ, the Lamb of God, is judged to be qualified to take possession of the deed to this earth. The redeeming work Christ completed two thousand years ago was essential to the eternal destiny of this world. "For God so loved the world, that he gave his only begotten Son, that whosoever believeth in him should not perish, but have everlasting life" (John 3:16).

We know from Scripture that God foresaw the fall of humanity into sin. Foreseeing humanity's fall, God devised a plan to save them even before this world was created. This is why Revelation refers to Christ as "the Lamb slain from the foundation of the world" (Revelation 13:8). As soon as there was sin, there was a Savior. This is also why God could promise Adam and Eve that they would be saved, while at the same time telling the serpent, Satan: "I will put enmity between thee and the woman, and between thy seed and her seed; it shall bruise thy head, and thou shalt bruise his heel" (Genesis 3:15).

God also foretold in the Old Testament that the time would come when the Holy Spirit would become available to fill every believer; not just a few as was the case before Christ completed His work of redemption. Through the prophet Joel God prophesied the coming of the Holy Spirit in power: "Ye shall know that I am in the midst of Israel, and that I am the LORD your God, and none else: and my people shall never be ashamed. And it shall come to pass afterward, that I will pour out my spirit upon all flesh; and your sons and your daughters shall prophesy, your old men shall dream dreams, your young men shall see visions: And also upon the servants and upon the handmaids in those days will I pour out my spirit" (Joel 2:27–29).

God said that after the "I AM"—Jesus Christ (see John 8:58) — appeared in Israel, God would "pour out" His "spirit upon all flesh." By "all flesh," God meant all believers; not just a few as had been the case in the Old Testament era. When, on the day of Pentecost, Peter explained what was happening, he said it was the fulfillment of Joel's prophecy (see Acts 2:16–21).

Dominion over this world had been returned to humankind in the person of Jesus Christ because by His righteous life, His death on the cross, and His resurrection, Jesus had defeated Satan. That opened the way for the Holy Spirit to be poured out and made Him fully available so He could fill every believer in Jesus Christ. This is the experience in the Spirit to

which Jesus was referring when He said, "I will pray the Father, and he shall give you another Comforter, that he may abide with you for ever; even the Spirit of truth; whom the world cannot receive, because it seeth him not, neither knoweth him: but ye know him; for he dwelleth with you, and shall be in you" (John 14:16, 17).

It is important to note that Jesus clearly stated that this experience was not available to everyone in the world; only those who were followers of Jesus. This great blessing in the Spirit is available to every Christian today. In fact, Christ's followers must have this infilling of the Spirit so God's work can be completed in their lives and the world can be prepared for Christ's second coming.

Discussion Questions

1. **What did Satan gain when Adam yielded to his temptation?**

2. **How was the Holy Spirit limited in the Old Testament times?**

3. **When, according to Joel, would the limitation of the Holy Spirit end?**

4. **What experience in the Spirit became available after the Crucifixion?**

5. **Why did Christ's victory on the cross allow the Holy Spirit to be poured out on all believers?**

Prayer Focus
Pray for:

- **God to fill you with the Holy Spirit.**
- **Those on your prayer list.**

Day 8

The Cross and the Baptism of the Holy Spirit

In yesterday's devotional we saw that because of Adam's sin, Satan took from Adam the dominion in this world that God had given him. When Satan gained the dominion in this world that had been Adam and Eve's, the work of the Holy Spirit was somewhat limited. The Holy Spirit wasn't available to all of God's people in the way He has been since His outpouring after Jesus' resurrection. Because of Adam's fall, in Old Testament times, only those believers whom God called to do for a special work—people such as Moses and the prophets—could be filled with the Spirit.

This all changed when Jesus came and gained the victory over Satan. For Jesus to be victorious, it was essential that He be filled with the Spirit at the beginning of His ministry. He was when He was baptized by John the Baptist. Scripture says, "Now when all the people were baptized, it came to pass, that Jesus also being baptized, and praying, the heaven was opened, and the Holy Ghost descended in a bodily shape like a dove upon him, and a voice came from heaven, which said, Thou art my beloved Son; in thee I am well pleased" (Luke 3:21, 22).

In answer to His prayer, the Father baptized Jesus with the Holy Spirit. The Spirit's baptism was essential to Christ's daily victory over Satan. Of this, Ellen White wrote, "Daily He received a fresh baptism of the Holy Spirit. In the early hours of the new day the Lord awakened Him from His slumbers, and His soul and His lips were anointed with grace, that He might impart to others. His words were given Him fresh from the heavenly courts, words that He might speak in season to the weary and oppressed" (*Christ's Object Lessons*, p. 139).

Immediately following Christ's Spirit baptism we find Him in the wilderness facing His greatest temptations. He wasn't ready for those temptations until He was filled with the Spirit. Once filled with the Spirit, He was then ready to do combat with the archenemy of God. The same is true of Christians today. We aren't ready to face Satan's greatest temptations until we, too, are filled with the Spirit. As with Christ, we also must be filled anew every day with the Spirit.

Christ knew that His victory over Satan and His death on the cross would make the Holy Spirit available to every believer. Because the Spirit's infilling was so essential for the believers' growth into the fullness of Christ and their achieving victory over Satan's temptations, Christ was eager for the Spirit's outpouring. We can sense that eagerness when we read, "I have come to bring fire on the earth, and how I wish it were already kindled!" (Luke 12:49, NIV).

In the next verse, Jesus referred to the cross and everything else associated with the suffering that He must endure for the Spirit to be poured out in fullness. He said, "I have a baptism to undergo, and what constraint I am under until it is completed!" (verse 50, NIV). Jesus' daily encounters with Satan; the temptations He faced; the constant criticism of the Pharisees; His arrest in the Garden of Gethsemane; the fleeing of His disciples; the mock trial; and the cross with its humiliation, shame; and His Father's apparent turning away from Him because of our sins were difficult for Jesus to endure. But endure He did because He loves us and wants us with Him forever.

Jesus knew that once His followers were filled with the Spirit, His presence would abide with them

27

and they would carry out a great ministry. Concerning the Spirit and Christ's presence, Ellen White wrote, "The work of the holy Spirit is immeasurably great. It is from this source that power and efficiency come to the worker for God; and the holy Spirit is the comforter, *as the personal presence of Christ* to the soul" (*Review and Herald,* Nov. 29, 1892; emphasis added. See also John 14:16–18).

Christ foretold the powerful ministry of His followers, saying, "He that believeth on me, as the scripture hath said, out of his belly shall flow rivers of living water" (John 7:38). John clarified what Jesus was referring to, telling us, "This spake he of the Spirit, which they that believe on him should receive: for the Holy Ghost was not yet given; because that Jesus was not yet glorified" (verse 39). These "rivers of living water" would bring life to all who chose to accept the gospel of Jesus Christ that every believer would proclaim in power following the Day of Pentecost when the baptism of the Holy Spirit became available to every believer.

It is because of the cross of Christ that Satan's defeat was complete and the baptism of the Holy Spirit could then be experienced by every follower of Jesus Christ. Christ has, at great cost to Himself, made the baptism and infilling of the Spirit available to us. May no Christian neglect to receive that baptism and infilling every day. Paul actually commands us to "be not drunk with wine, wherein is excess; but be filled with the Spirit" (Ephesians 5:18). The Greek word translated "be filled" is a continuous action verb meaning "keep on being filled." We must pray every day for the infilling of the Holy Spirit if we want to grow into the fullness of Christ and be victorious over Satan.

Discussion Questions

1. **What experience in the Spirit did Christ have to receive daily in order to be victorious over Satan?**

   _____

2. **According to Ellen White, how often was Christ baptized with the Spirit?** _____

   _____

3. **What experience in the Spirit was Christ anticipating eagerly?** _____

   _____

4. **What did Christ do that allowed the Holy Spirit to be poured out on the Day of Pentecost?**

   _____

5. **Why must every believer receive the baptism of the Holy Spirit?** _____

   _____

6. **What does Paul command us to do concerning the Holy Spirit?** _____

   _____

Prayer Focus
Pray for:

- **God to fill you with the Holy Spirit.**
- **God to help you realize the price Christ paid for you to be able to be baptized with the Spirit.**
- **Those on your prayer list.**

The Blessings of the
Cross

Day 9

The Cross and Justification by Faith

According to the Bible every human being on planet earth is a sinner: "As it is written, There is none righteous, no, not one. . . . For all have sinned, and come short of the glory of God" (Romans 3:10, 23). Because of this sinful condition, humankind justly deserves the death sentence God has pronounced on them—"for the wages of sin is death" (Romans 6:23).

However, God declared in His heart, "I love you so much that I refuse to let you go." So before Adam and Eve were created, even before the creation of this world, God devised a plan to save them. He knew the cost of saving humanity from sin would be high, and it was. The plan was that He would die in the sinners' place.

So that Christ could become our substitute, the Lord "laid on him the iniquity of us all" (Isaiah 53:6). Christ bore our sins on the cross and died the death we deserve. As a result of His sacrifice on the cross on our behalf we can be forgiven, escape the death penalty, and receive eternal life. The apostle John wrote: "This is the record, that God hath given to us eternal life, and this life is in his Son. He that hath the Son hath life; and he that hath not the Son of God hath not life. These things have I written unto you that believe on the name of the Son of God; that ye may know that ye have eternal life, and that ye may believe on the name of the Son of God" (1 John 5:11–13).

As a result of what Christ did for us on the cross we can be justified. By definition, to be justified is to be declared free from the guilt and penalty of lawbreaking. When you place your faith in Christ, you are cleared of the guilt and penalty of your sins. You stand justified before God.

God's forgiveness is so complete that He states,

"Their sins and their iniquities will I remember no more" (Hebrews 8:12). Satan may tempt you to doubt this promise of God, but consider what God did for David.

Though David should have known better, he committed adultery with Bathsheba and then ordered the murder of Uriah, Bathsheba's husband. Despite these terrible sins, when David repented, God forgave him. This forgiveness was so complete that when God was chastising rebellious King Jeroboam, He used David as an example of faithfulness! God ordered the prophet to tell Jeroboam, "Thus saith the LORD God of Israel, Forasmuch as I exalted thee from among the people, and made thee prince over my people Israel, and rent the kingdom away from the house of David, and gave it thee: and yet thou hast not been as my servant David, *who kept my commandments, and who followed me with all his heart, to do that only which was right in mine eyes*" (1 Kings 14:7, 8; emphasis added).

Later, God chose David and Bathsheba's son Solomon to become the next king in the Messianic line. (See 2 Samuel 12.) No doubt there were many people whom God could have chosen to follow David and Solomon in that line, so we might ask why He would choose those He did? God can do such things because Jesus' death on the cross justified God's extending amazing grace and complete forgiveness to sinners.

God gives something else to sinners when they accept Jesus Christ as their Savior. Christ resisted temptations and lived a perfectly sinless, obedient, righteous life on our behalf. He offers this righteousness to sinners who accept Him as their Savior, "for he hath made him to be sin for us, who knew no sin;

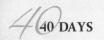

that we might be made the righteousness of God in him" (2 Corinthians 5:21).

The apostle Paul expressed this well when he wrote that his desire was to be "found in him [Christ], not having mine own righteousness, which is of the law, but that which is through the faith of Christ, the righteousness which is of God by faith" (Philippians 3:9). God offers this same righteousness to all. God calls us to accept Christ as our Savior, become free from the guilt and penalty of our sin, and be declared righteous in the sight of God—covered with Christ's righteousness. It is the cross of Christ that has made this experience available to the sinner. Ellen White stated this clearly. She said, "Christ was treated as we deserve, that we might be treated as He deserves. He was condemned for our sins, in which He had no share, that we might be justified by His righteousness, in which we had no share. He suffered the death which was ours, that we might receive the life which was His. 'With His stripes we are healed' " (*The Desire of Ages,* p. 25).

Discussion Questions

1. **What does it mean to be justified?** _____

   _____

2. **What kind of life did Jesus live?** _____

   _____

3. **What is the only way one can become righteous in God's sight?** _____

   _____

4. **What kind of righteousness did Paul desire?** _____

   _____

5. **How complete is God's forgiveness of the sinner? Give an example.** _____

   _____

6. **How did Ellen White describe what Christ does for those who believe in Him?** _____

   _____

Prayer Focus

Pray for:

- **God to fill you with the Holy Spirit.**
- **God to forgive you for your sins, and to free you from the guilt and penalty of your sins, and to cover you with Christ's righteousness.**
- **Those on your prayer list.**

Day 10

The Cross and Sanctification by Faith—Part 1

In today's devotional we will consider how Christians are to experience sanctification by faith in Christ to become free from the power of sin in their life. The apostle Paul understood the gospel of victory over sin. He wrote, "What shall we say then? Shall we continue in sin, that grace may abound? God forbid. How shall we, that are dead to sin, live any longer therein?" (Romans 6:1, 2). Here Paul clearly states that the followers of Jesus Christ should not be living lives of habitual sin. He then goes on to explain why this is so.

Know ye not, that so many of us as were baptized into Jesus Christ were baptized into his death? Therefore we are buried with him by baptism into death: that like as Christ was raised up from the dead by the glory of the Father, even so we also should walk in newness of life. For if we have been planted together in the likeness of his death, we shall be also in the likeness of his resurrection: Knowing this, that our old man is crucified with him, that the body of sin might be destroyed, that henceforth we should not serve sin. For he that is dead is freed from sin (Romans 6:3–7).

In these verses Paul is telling us that all who have accepted Jesus Christ died with Him on the cross and were buried with Him in the grave. Therefore, the old sinful-nature you, the sin-loving you, the prideful you, the unforgiving you, the angry you, the lustful you, is dead and buried with Christ. Since your old sinful nature is dead and buried, it need not control you any longer.

So when you are tempted to sin, you are to believe that the old sinful nature that once controlled you need not control you anymore, and you do not need to yield to the temptation to sin. At the moment of temptation you put that sinful you back on the cross and believe that it dies and is buried with Christ. This is what it means to "die daily" and to "take up your cross daily."

Knowing this to be a fact and that you don't have to live the old life of sin, Paul goes on to write:

Now if we be dead with Christ, we believe that we shall also live with him: Knowing that Christ being raised from the dead dieth no more; death hath no more dominion over him. For in that he died, he died unto sin once: but in that he liveth, he liveth unto God. Likewise reckon ye also yourselves to be dead indeed unto sin, but alive unto God through Jesus Christ our Lord. Let not sin therefore reign in your mortal body, that ye should obey it in the lusts thereof. Neither yield ye your members as instruments of unrighteousness unto sin: but yield yourselves unto God, as those that are alive from the dead, and your members as instruments of righteousness unto God. For sin shall not have dominion over you: for ye are not under the law, but under grace (Romans 6:8–14).

In his letter to the Galatians, Paul uses himself as an example to describe how the Christian is to live an obedient life through Christ. Paul writes, "I am crucified with Christ: nevertheless I live; yet not I, but Christ liveth in me: and the life which I now live in the flesh I

live by the faith of the Son of God, who loved me, and gave himself for me" (Galatians 2:20).

First, Paul accepted the fact that he was "crucified with Christ." The old sinful Paul was dead and buried with Christ. Then he is quick to point out that he's still alive, but he wasn't actually living on his own and controlling his life. Rather, he says that it's not really him who is alive; it's Christ living in him.

Paul regarded Christ's living in him to be a reality—one in which he depended on Christ for victory over sin. When he says he lives by "the faith of the Son of God,"

he means the Son of God's faithful obedience to His Father. So, what Paul is saying is that he lives the obedient Christian life by depending on faith in Christ, who is living in him, to continue to live a life of obedience to His Father in and through Paul. So Paul's obedience was actually Christ's righteous obedience manifest in and through him. This is the true biblical experience of sanctification by faith in Christ alone. Christ's righteousness is "imparted." In other words, it becomes the believer's life. It can become a reality in your life because of the cross of Christ.

Discussion Questions

1. **How would you define sanctification by faith?** _____
    _____

2. **What kind of life did Paul call Christians to live?** _____
    _____

3. **What happened to the sinful people who believed in Christ when He died on the cross?** _____
    _____

4. **How did Paul describe his life in Christ?** _____
    _____

5. **Whose righteousness did Paul depend on in order to live an obedient life?** _____
    _____

Prayer Focus
Pray for:

- **God to fill you with the Holy Spirit.**
- **Christ to live out His life of obedience in you.**
- **Those on your prayer list.**

Day 11

The Cross and Sanctification by Faith—Part 2

In yesterday's devotional we reviewed the biblical truth that sin's control of believers was broken at the cross because those who believe in Jesus Christ were crucified with Him. Therefore, the old sinful-nature you, the sin-loving you, the prideful you, the unforgiving you, the angry you, the lustful you, is dead and buried with Christ. Thus your old sinful nature is dead and buried and need not control you any longer. In today's devotional, we will consider how Christians are to apply this truth to their everyday life.

In order to have the victory God wants us to have, we must keep our eyes on Christ constantly—or, as Paul puts it, we must "pray without ceasing" (1 Thessalonians 5:17). We must diligently seek to be led by the Spirit moment by moment, and we must be sensitive to the Spirit's conviction when temptation comes our way. This will require 100 percent complete surrender of self 100 percent of the time. This is what Paul meant when he said, "I die daily" (1 Corinthians 15:31), and it is also what Christ meant when He said, "If any man will come after me, let him deny himself, and take up his cross daily, and follow me" (Luke 9:23).

You see, our sinful nature will try to dominate us. It will cry out for us to satisfy it by yielding to temptation. Our part in avoiding this is to choose to turn away from the temptation; to "deny self," to "take up our cross," to "die" to the yearning to satisfy the temptation, and to look to Christ, asking Him to give us His victory over this temptation, and to believe that He will do just that. You see, all we can do is choose and believe. We choose by giving our will to God, and then we must believe that Christ will give us His victory. This is the experience those will have who receive the latter rain and are ready for Christ's return.

You may find yourself having a desire for a particular sin that you really don't want to give up. In that case, look to Jesus. Ask Him to give you the response that He wants you to have concerning that particular sin, for Jesus not only gives us forgiveness for sin, but also repentance—a changed attitude toward that sin; a desire to avoid it (see Acts 5:31). Concerning this, Ellen White wrote:

The victory is not won without much earnest prayer, without the humbling of self at every step. Our will is not to be forced into co-operation with divine agencies, but it must be voluntarily submitted. Were it possible to force upon you with a hundredfold greater intensity the influence of the Spirit of God, it would not make you a Christian, a fit subject for heaven. The stronghold of Satan would not be broken. The will must be placed on the side of God's will. You are not able, of yourself, to bring your purposes and desires and inclinations into submission to the will of God; but if you are "willing to be made willing," God will accomplish the work for you, even "casting down imaginations, and every high thing that exalteth itself against the knowledge of God, and bringing into captivity every thought to the obedience of Christ." 2 Corinthians 10:5. Then you will "work out your own salvation with fear and trembling. For it is God which worketh in you both to will and to do of His good pleasure." Philippians 2:12, 13. (*Thoughts From the Mount of Blessing,* p. 142).

Similarly, she wrote,

35

The only defense against evil is the indwelling of Christ in the heart through faith in His righteousness. Unless we become vitally connected with God, we can never resist the unhallowed effects of self-love, self-indulgence, and temptation to sin. We may leave off many bad habits, for the time we may part company with Satan; but without a vital connection with God, through the surrender of ourselves to Him moment by moment, we shall be overcome. Without a personal acquaintance with Christ, and a continual communion, we are at the mercy of the enemy, and shall do his bidding in the end (*The Desire of Ages,* p. 324).

This issue is at the heart of the gospel and the message of righteousness by faith. The Bible is clear on the matter. Concerning the Christian's walk with God, Paul wrote: "As ye have therefore received Christ Jesus the Lord, so walk ye in him" (Colossians 2:6). The way we receive Jesus Christ as our justifying Savior is by faith. We believe that Jesus is the Son of God, that He died for our sins, that He forgives our sins, and that He gives us eternal life. We become Christians by faith in Christ. Works are not involved.

God doesn't require lost sinners to begin doing good works before they come to Christ. Sinners don't have to clean up their life to make themselves acceptable to God before they receive salvation. No, sinners simply come to Christ as they are, and they accept Him by faith as their Savior—they accept what Christ has done for them.

The same principle of faith applies to the sanctification of Christians; their living the obedient life. When tempted, Christians are simply to place their faith in Christ, to live out His obedient, righteous life within themselves. "Wherefore seeing we also are compassed about with so great a cloud of witnesses, let us lay aside every weight, and the sin which doth so easily beset us, and let us run with patience the race that is set before us, looking unto Jesus the author and finisher of our faith" (Hebrews 12:1, 2).

Discussion Questions

1. **What does "pray without ceasing" mean?** _____

2. **What did Christ mean when He said, "Take up your cross daily and follow me"?** _____ _____

3. **What should you do if you really don't want to give up a particular sin?** _____ _____

4. **When you are tempted, what should you do to attain victory over the temptation?** _____ _____

5. **According to Hebrews 12:1, 2, what kind of life are Christians to live, and how are they to live that life?** _____ _____

Prayer Focus
Pray for:

- **God to fill you with the Holy Spirit.**
- **God to give you—when you are tempted—the desire to obey Him and to remind you to depend on Jesus to give you His obedience.**
- **Those on your prayer list.**

Day 12

The Cross and Deliverance

Humans were created to live in the Garden of Eden, where there was no sickness, emotional pain, or death. Humanity was designed to be physically healthy, living forever; emotionally healthy, with no emotional wounds; and spiritually healthy, with an intimate relationship with God. As we know from Scripture, humans didn't continue in this wonderful condition for very long. When Adam and Eve chose to sin, they lost everything. The curse of sin began to ravage the human race. The earth itself brought forth thorns and thistles. Cain, Adam and Eve's first son, murdered Abel, Adam and Eve's second son. As the centuries passed, disease and sickness began appearing in the human race. The sinful desires that controlled humankind damaged their relationships, and they wandered farther and farther away from God. Because of Adam and Eve's sin, the entire human race came under the curse of God.

As we have seen in the devotions we've already studied, God devised a plan to save humans from their sinful condition. God's plan was to make it possible for humans to escape the ultimate consequences of their sins. God was to come to this earth in the person of Jesus Christ and become a substitute for sinful humanity, suffer for humanity's sin, pay the price for humanity's sins, and provide deliverance for sinful humankind.

Humans can be delivered from the spiritual consequences of their sin by accepting Christ as their Savior. This deliverance is possible because Christ allowed Himself to be tempted in all points as we are, and won the victory over those temptations for us (see Hebrews 4:15). He developed a perfect human righteousness for us. He then allowed "the LORD [to lay] on him the iniquity of us all" (Isaiah 53:6). Jesus bore our sins on the cross, and He died the death of a God-forsaken sinner for us. When we accept Jesus Christ as our Savior, we can then be forgiven for our sins, receive eternal life, and have Christ's righteousness imputed to us, enabling us to stand in Christ's righteousness before God. Christ made it possible for us to have the eternal relationship with God we were created to have.

Also, when Christ lives within Christians, they can have victory over sinful temptations by depending on Him to give His victory to them. Paul described this when he wrote to the Galatians: "I am crucified with Christ: nevertheless I live; yet not I, but Christ liveth in me: and the life which I now live in the flesh I live by the faith of the Son of God, who loved me, and gave himself for me" (Galatians 2:20).

Jesus also paid the price to deliver us from the physical consequences of our sin. In Matthew, we read: "When the even was come, they brought unto him many that were possessed with devils: and he cast out the spirits with his word, and healed all that were sick: That it might be fulfilled which was spoken by Esaias the prophet, saying, Himself took our infirmities, and bare our sicknesses" (Matthew 8:16, 17). Jesus can heal humans of sickness and disease because while He was on the cross He took upon Himself our sickness and disease. This is why James could instruct Christians; "Is any sick among you? let him call for the elders of the church; and let them pray over him, anointing him with oil in the name of the Lord: And the prayer of faith shall save the sick, and the Lord shall raise him up; and if he have committed sins, they

shall be forgiven him" (James 5:14, 15). On the cross Jesus paid the price for our physical healing.

The suffering that Christ endured also made it possible for us to be healed of the consequences of sin seen in our damaged emotions. Humanity's sinful condition has resulted in the heart bearing many wounds because of physical abuse, emotional abuse (such as children being told "You are stupid," and "You will never amount to anything"), sexual abuse, and religious abuse. Christ suffered each of these terrible abuses Himself—thus paying the price for our healing. He overcame the emotional pain of being alone and abandoned in the Garden of Gethsemane and on the cross. He suffered the emotional pain of betrayal when Judas sold Him for thirty pieces of silver. Christ suffered physical abuse at His mockery of a trial, when He was spat upon, slapped in the face, and beaten with a metal-barbed whip. He suffered verbal abuse when He was blindfolded, mocked, and ridiculed. And religious abuse was heaped on Him by the religious leaders. As Christ hung naked on the cross, He suffered the shame of sexual abuse. He overcame the temptation to take a drug to deaden the pain He was experiencing. Christ suffered terrible abuses in order to gain the victory over them for us. He paid the price so He could deliver us from the wounds we have experienced due to such abuse.

Because of Christ's suffering and death on the cross, He can deliver us from the consequences of sin. Because of the deliverance Jesus provides for His people, God "will dwell with them, and they shall be his people, and God himself shall be with them, and be their God. And God shall wipe away all tears from their eyes; and there shall be no more death, neither sorrow, nor crying, neither shall there be any more pain: for the former things are passed away" (Revelation 21:3, 4).

Discussion Questions

1. What kind of environment were humans created to live in? _____

2. How did sin change humanity's spiritual relationship with God? _____

3. How did sin affect humanity's physical condition? _____

4. How did sin affect humanity's emotions? _____

5. How did Christ make it possible for humans to be delivered from the spiritual, physical, and emotional consequences of sin? _____

Prayer Focus

Pray for:

- God to fill you with the Holy Spirit.
- God to lead you to experience the full deliverance Jesus paid for you to have.
- Those on your prayer list.

Day 13

The Cross and Christ's Second Coming

Throughout the ages, Christians have looked forward to the second coming of Christ. When Christ met with His disciples during the forty days following His resurrection, they were eager to know when He would establish His kingdom. They asked Him, "Lord, wilt thou at this time restore again the kingdom to Israel?" (Acts 1:6). Paul stated that all Christians who live godly lives are "looking for that blessed hope, and the glorious appearing of the great God and our Saviour Jesus Christ" (Titus 2:13).

The second coming of Christ will affect every man and woman on planet earth. It will be no secret event, for John has told us: "Behold, he cometh with clouds; and every eye shall see him, and they also which pierced him: and all kindreds of the earth shall wail because of him. Even so, Amen" (Revelation 1:7).

The day of Christ's return will be a very fearful day for those who have rejected Him. They will try to hide themselves from Him. "The kings of the earth, and the great men, and the rich men, and the chief captains, and the mighty men, and every bondman, and every free man, hid themselves in the dens and in the rocks of the mountains; and said to the mountains and rocks, Fall on us, and hide us from the face of him that sitteth on the throne, and from the wrath of the Lamb: for the great day of his wrath is come; and who shall be able to stand?" (Revelation 6:15–17).

Christ's second coming will bring destruction to all who have chosen to reject God's truth and refused God's call to repent and accept Christ as their Savior. Paul describes their destruction in these words:

Then shall that Wicked be revealed, whom the Lord shall consume with the spirit of his mouth, and shall destroy with the brightness of his coming: even him, whose coming is after the working of Satan with all power and signs and lying wonders, and with all deceivableness of unrighteousness in them that perish; because they received not the love of the truth, that they might be saved. And for this cause God shall send them strong delusion, that they should believe a lie: that they all might be damned who believed not the truth, but had pleasure in unrighteousness (2 Thessalonians 2:8–12).

Why can God's people survive the world-shaking event of Christ's second coming, which destroys everyone but them? Why aren't they killed too?

The answer is found in the cross of Christ. When Jesus died on the cross, all who have accepted Him as their Savior died with Him and were buried with Him.

Know ye not, that so many of us as were baptized into Jesus Christ were baptized into his death? Therefore we are buried with him by baptism into death: that like as Christ was raised up from the dead by the glory of the Father, even so we also should walk in newness of life. For if we have been planted together in the likeness of his death, we shall be also in the likeness of his resurrection: Knowing this, that our old man is crucified with him, that the body of sin might be destroyed, that henceforth we should not serve sin. For he that is dead is freed from sin. Now if we be dead with Christ, we believe that we shall also live with him (Romans 6:3–8).

Remember, when Christ died on the cross, He bore the curse and the wrath of God that was due all those who accept Him as their Savior. "Christ hath redeemed us from the curse of the law, being made a curse for us: for it is written, Cursed is every one that hangeth on a tree" (Galatians 3:13).

John described the destruction that those who have rejected Christ will experience. He said, "The angel thrust in his sickle into the earth, and gathered the vine of the earth, and cast it into the great winepress of the wrath of God. And the winepress was trodden without [outside of] the city [Jerusalem]" (Revelation 14:19, 20). Those lost will be destroyed by the brightness of Jesus' second coming. He had already suffered God's wrath when He was on the cross outside the "gate" of Jerusalem for His people (Hebrews 13:12).

So, why can God's people survive the second coming of Christ while everyone else on earth is being destroyed? They will survive because they have already died with Christ on the cross and were buried with Him. In Christ, they have already suffered the wrath He experienced for them outside the gate of Jerusalem on the cross. They are eternally free from the guilt and penalty of their sins, for Jesus paid the price for their freedom on the cross. As Paul wrote, "If we be dead with Christ, we believe that we shall also live with him" (Romans 6:8). You, too, can look forward to the second coming of Christ with rejoicing because you have accepted Christ as your Savior.

Discussion Questions

1. **How many human beings will Christ's second coming affect?** _____

    _____

2. **How do those who have rejected Christ as their Savior respond to His second coming?** _____

    _____

3. **What does the Bible say will happen to those who have rejected Christ as their Savior when He returns?** _____

4. **What constitutes the "suffering outside Jerusalem's gate" that Jesus did for His people?** ____

    _____

5. **What prevents the destruction of those who have accepted Christ as their Savior at the Second Coming?** _____

Prayer Focus

Pray for:

- **God to fill you with the Holy Spirit.**
- **God to give you the desire to renew your relationship with Christ every day and thus to be ready for His second coming.**
- **Those on your prayer list.**

The Disciples and the Cross

Day 14

The Disciples' Blindness and the Cross

The Bible tells us that spiritual things are "spiritually discerned" (see 1 Corinthians 2:13). On one occasion Peter declared who Christ was: "Thou art the Christ, the Son of the living God. And Jesus answered and said unto him, Blessed art thou, Simon Barjona: for flesh and blood hath not revealed it unto thee, but my Father which is in heaven" (Matthew 16:16, 17). It is only as the Holy Spirit opens our understanding to spiritual things that we can see and accept the teachings of God and the truths of His Word.

In Christ's day, most Jews believed that when the Messiah appeared He would overthrow the enemies of Israel and establish Israel as a great kingdom on earth. The scholars and teachers focused on the glorious kingdom prophecies of the Old Testament and applied them to the Messiah's appearance. They were blind to the "suffering servant" prophecies such as Isaiah 53 and to the focus of the earthly sanctuary and its services on the sacrifice that must be made for the forgiveness of people's sins. Since the disciples were children of their time, they were strongly influenced by this popular interpretation of Scripture. Even John the Baptist, whom Jesus called the greatest of the prophets (Matthew 11:11) and whom God had called to prepare the way for the Messiah and who had even pointed to Jesus as the Lamb of God, was seduced by these faulty applications of the Messianic prophecies in the Old Testament. John found these faulty applications of the Old Testament prophecies so attractive that when he was in prison, he sent his disciples to Jesus for His response to John's question "Art thou he that should come, or do we look for another?" (verse 3).

On several occasions Jesus told His disciples what was going to happen to Him—that He would be killed and then resurrected on the third day. "And they were all amazed at the mighty power of God. But while they wondered every one at all things which Jesus did, he said unto his disciples, Let these sayings sink down into your ears: for the Son of man shall be delivered into the hands of men. But they understood not this saying, and it was hid from them, that they perceived it not: and they feared to ask him of that saying" (Luke 9:43–45).

"Then he took unto him the twelve, and said unto them, Behold, we go up to Jerusalem, and all things that are written by the prophets concerning the Son of man shall be accomplished. For he shall be delivered unto the Gentiles, and shall be mocked, and spitefully entreated, and spitted on: And they shall scourge him, and put him to death: and the third day he shall rise again. And they understood none of these things: and this saying was hid from them, neither knew they the things which were spoken" (Luke 18:31–34).

In these scriptural references we find that the twelve whom Jesus had personally selected to be His disciples as well as John the Baptist were blind to the cross of Christ. It appears the disciples were focused on worldly greatness, for we are told that right after Jesus warned the disciples of what was going to happen to Him "there arose a reasoning among them, which of them should be greatest" (Luke 9:46).

The same danger awaits every Christian today—the danger of focusing on worldly wealth and greatness. If our primary focus is directed at this world, we, too, shall be blind to many spiritual truths. Jesus said,

Lay not up for yourselves treasures upon earth, where moth and rust doth corrupt, and where thieves break through and steal: But lay up for yourselves treasures in heaven, where neither moth nor rust doth corrupt, and where thieves do not break through nor steal: For where your treasure is, there will your heart be also. The light of the body is the eye: if therefore thine eye be single, thy whole body shall be full of light. But if thine eye be evil, thy whole body shall be full of darkness. If therefore the light that is in thee be darkness, how great is that darkness! Matthew 6:19–23.

Christians whose focus is primarily on the world will not be as full of light as God desires them to be. So it is imperative that we learn the lesson of the disciples' blindness to the cross. May we each "seek . . . first the kingdom of God, and his righteousness" (Matthew 6:33). Jesus said that if we do, then "all these things shall be added unto [us]" (verse 33). If our primary focus is on God and spiritual things, we will have all the necessities of life, and we won't be blind to what lies ahead—which is so essential in these last days.

Discussion Questions

1. **What was the popular belief concerning what the Messiah would do when He appeared in Israel?**

   _____

2. **How did this belief influence John the Baptist and the twelve disciples?** _____

   _____

3. **Did Jesus warn His disciples ahead of time that He would be crucified and then raised on the third day? What was their response?** _____

4. **What will be the effect on our spiritual insight and understanding of directing our primary focus to worldly things?** _____

   _____

Prayer Focus

Pray for:

- **God to fill you with His Spirit.**
- **God to help you focus on spiritual things and to remove any spiritual blindness you may have.**
- **Those on your prayer list.**

Day 15

The Disciples' Fear and the Cross

Jesus warned the disciples about what was going to happen to Him. "Then he took unto him the twelve, and said unto them, Behold, we go up to Jerusalem, and all things that are written by the prophets concerning the Son of man shall be accomplished. For he shall be delivered unto the Gentiles, and shall be mocked, and spitefully entreated, and spitted on: And they shall scourge him, and put him to death: and the third day he shall rise again. And they understood none of these things: and this saying was hid from them, neither knew they the things which were spoken" (Luke 18:31–34).

As we saw in the previous day's devotional, the disciples' primary focus was on worldly greatness, and that blinded them to seeing the truth of what Jesus was telling them. The psalmist declared that God's truth "shall be thy shield and buckler" (Psalm 91:4). If the disciples had understood the truth that Jesus was revealing to them, they would have been prepared for the terrible events connected with His crucifixion. However, since their focus was on this world, they didn't understand what Jesus was saying, and consequently, they feared the Jews (see John 20:19). They were afraid they would suffer the same fate as Jesus apparently had.

Fear is the opposite of faith. God wants every Christian to place his or her faith in His Word. It contains His promises, which He gave to sustain His people when times are difficult. Satan is constantly seeking to lead God's people to doubt His Word. Following him will always lead to fear. Paul tells us that faith is an essential part of the armor God has provided to enable us to gain the victory over Satan. He names

as most important "the shield of faith," with which, he says, we will be able to "quench all the fiery darts of the wicked" (Ephesians 6:16). In other words, faith is the shield God gives us to protect us from Satan's temptations to doubt God's Word. If our shield is small because we haven't developed it, many of Satan's "fiery darts" will get through to harm us spiritually, emotionally, and even physically.

You see, the truth is that when we doubt God's Word, we are saying, "God, You are a liar; and Satan, you are telling the truth." Doubt will lead us to believe the devil's lies and to reject God's promises. And Satan has the right to attack us regarding those things that we fear, because our doubts mean we don't have faith, so it doesn't protect us regarding that matter. Job said, "The thing which I greatly feared is come upon me, and that which I was afraid of is come unto me. I was not in safety, neither had I rest, neither was I quiet; yet trouble came" (Job 3:25, 26). The New International Version's translation of verse 26 reads, "I have no peace, no quietness; I have no rest, but only turmoil." That's the result of doubting God's promises.

The disciple John understood this too. He wrote, "Fear hath torment. He that feareth is not made perfect in love" (1 John 4:18). The torment caused by fear robs Christians of the peace God wants His children to have. Satan knows that the "joy of the LORD is [our] strength" (Nehemiah 8:10). When we fear, we lose our joy, which greatly weakens us and makes us much more vulnerable to Satan's attacks.

God inspired Isaiah to tell us how we can keep peace in our heart under all circumstances. Isaiah wrote, "Thou wilt keep him in perfect peace, whose

mind is stayed on thee: because he trusteth in thee" (Isaiah 26:3). The key to keeping peace and faith in God in our hearts is to keep our minds focused on God and His Word. This truth is taught throughout the Bible. God counseled Joshua as he faced a daunting task after Moses's death: "This book of the law shall not depart out of thy mouth; but thou shalt meditate therein day and night, that thou mayest observe to do according to all that is written therein: for then thou shalt make thy way prosperous, and then thou shalt have good success. Have not I commanded thee? Be strong and of a good courage; be not afraid, neither be thou dismayed: for the LORD thy God is with thee whithersoever thou goest" (Joshua 1:8, 9). This promise is true for every Christian today as well. If we meditate on God's Word throughout the day, keeping our eyes on Jesus, we will be strong in the Lord, have good courage, and fear nothing. May we learn the lesson of the disciples' fear and the cross.

Discussion Questions

1. **What warning did Jesus give to the disciples about what would happen to Him?** _____
   _____

2. **The disciples didn't understand Jesus' warning about His crucifixion. What did the disciples do because of their misunderstanding?** _____

3. **What is our shield against Satan's temptations to be fearful?** _____

4. **What does our fearfulness tell God? What does it tell Satan?** _____
   _____

5. **What feelings will we have if we are fearful?** _____

6. **What is the key to overcoming Satan's temptation to become fearful?** _____
   _____

Prayer Focus
Pray for:

- **God to fill you with His Spirit today.**
- **God to open your understanding to His promises and to give you the faith to believe them.**
- **Those on your prayer list.**

Day 16

The Disciples' Pride and the Cross

Pride has been a foundational part of the fallen nature of created beings ever since sin entered this universe. In spite of being created prefect, Lucifer allowed pride to dominate him. Of him, Isaiah wrote, "How art thou fallen from heaven, O Lucifer, son of the morning! how art thou cut down to the ground, which didst weaken the nations! For thou hast said in thine heart, I will ascend into heaven, I will exalt my throne above the stars of God: I will sit also upon the mount of the congregation, in the sides of the north: I will ascend above the heights of the clouds; I will be like the most High" (Isaiah 14:12–14).

Ever since the fall of humanity, pride has threatened to dominate people's every thought, word, and action. When Jesus called the disciples, they were no less sinful than were their neighbors. Like them, the disciples were filled with pride and self-seeking. On one occasion, James and John brought their mother to Jesus to request that in Jesus' kingdom, her sons be placed on His right hand and on His left hand—positions of authority. (See Matthew 22:20, 21.) This, of course, wasn't well received by the other disciples when they heard about it; "they were moved with indignation against the two brethren" (Matthew 20:24). They were moved with indignation because they, too, wanted to sit on the right hand and left hand of Jesus. They certainly would have liked to have made the same request to Jesus, but James, John, and their mother asked first.

The matter of who would hold the highest position in Christ's kingdom arose numerous times before His crucifixion. On one occasion, right after Jesus warned the disciples that He would be "delivered into the hands of men"—referring to His crucifixion—we are told "then there arose a reasoning among them, which of them should be greatest" (Luke 9:46). It is quite clear from the Gospel accounts that all of the disciples were filled with pride and self-seeking, which are dangerous sins to harbor in one's heart. Solomon warns, "Pride goeth before destruction, and an haughty spirit before a fall" (Proverbs 16:18). The truth is that God can't use anyone in any significant way while pride dominates one's spirit. James counseled, "Humble yourselves in the sight of the Lord, and he shall lift you up" (James 4:10). And Peter wrote, "God resisteth the proud, and giveth grace to the humble. Humble yourselves therefore under the mighty hand of God, that he may exalt you in due time" (1 Peter 5:5, 6).

God used the cross to humble Christ's disciples. Peter, who had boasted at the Passover meal that he would never deny his Lord, denied Him three times, just as Christ predicted he would, as he waited outside the judgment hall. We are told that when Peter realized what he had done, he "wept bitterly" (Matthew 26:75).

The other disciples were no more faithful to Jesus, for we are told "the doors were shut where the disciples were assembled for fear of the Jews" (John 20:19). As painful as it was, this breaking of the disciples' pride prepared them to receive the baptism of the Holy Spirit. God had to do that so He could use them in a mighty way following Christ's resurrection. People who are broken no longer desire to hold a high position or to receive accolades from men. The truth is that when people are broken, they feel unworthy to hold *any* position in God's service.

Concerning pride, Ellen White wrote: "It is the

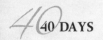

love of self that destroys our peace. While self is all alive, we stand ready continually to guard it from mortification and insult; but when we are dead, and our life is hid with Christ in God, we shall not take neglects or slights to heart. We shall be deaf to reproach and blind to scorn and insult" (*Thoughts From the Mount of Blessing,* p. 16).

The following paragraph pictures the actions and reactions people who are gaining the victory over pride will think and say and do. (Unfortunately, I don't know to whom this should be credited.)

When you are forgotten or neglected or purposely set at naught and you can smile inwardly, glorying in the insult or the oversight—*that is victory!* When your good is evil spoken of, when your wishes are crossed, your tastes offended, your advice disregarded, your opinions ridiculed and you take it all in patient and loving silence—*that is victory!* When you are content with any food and raiment, any climate and society, any solitude, and interruption—*that is victory!* When you can bear with any discord, any irregularity, any unpunctuality, any annoyance—*that is victory!* When you can stand face to face with waste, folly, extravagance, spiritual insensibility and endure it all as Jesus endured it—*that is victory!* When you never care to refer to yourself in conversation, or to record your own good works, or to seek after commendation, when you can truly love to be unknown—*that is victory!*

It is when we experience the humility of the cross that God can use us most gloriously in His cause; for then Christ—and only Christ—will be exalted.

Discussion Questions

1. **What filled Lucifer's heart and caused his fall?** _____

2. **What sinful trait led the disciples to desire to be the greatest in Christ's kingdom?** _____
_____

3. **How did the cross lead the disciples to overcome their pride?** _____
_____

4. **List some characteristics of an individual who has gained the victory over pride.** _____
_____

Prayer Focus
Pray for:

- **God to fill you with His Spirit.**
- **God to open your eyes to any pride that is in your heart.**
- **Those on your prayer list.**

The Seven Sayings of Christ on the Cross

Day 17

The First Saying of Christ on the Cross—Part 1

"And when they were come to the place, which is called Calvary, there they crucified him, and the malefactors, one on the right hand, and the other on the left. Then said Jesus, *Father, forgive them; for they know not what they do*" (Luke 23:33, 34).

God, the Creator of the world, came to the world He created. At His birth there was no place for him, King Herod tried to kill Him, and throughout His ministry His enemies sought to destroy Him. Finally, at the end of His earthly ministry, He surrendered Himself to the vilest of men, suffered a mock trial, was slandered, mocked, beaten, and finally crucified on the cross.

Notice the word *then*. *Then*—after Christ was brought to Calvary and crucified. *Then*—after His persecutors had severely brutalized Him and their evil hearts were revealed. *Then* . . .

Jesus could have threatened condemnation and revenge. As the song says, He could have called ten thousand angels to deliver Him. He could have wreaked His wrath on them and destroyed them all. But He didn't do any of that. Instead He spoke love—a divine love that had never before been so clearly revealed.

Then, as He hangs silent on the cross, instead of calling out for pity or cursing those who are crucifying Him, as He hang dying, He utters the words "Father, forgive them; for they know not what they do."

The first words we hear from Christ in His torment and pain on the cross are a prayer. His public ministry began with prayer at His baptism in water: "When all the people were baptized, it came to pass, that Jesus also being baptized, and praying, the heaven was opened" (Luke 3:21).

Throughout His ministry He prayed—sometimes all night, and with fasting. He prayed for strength for His mission. He prayed for His disciples. He prayed for the sick, He cast out devils with His word, and He even raised the dead. Now His hands could no longer minister to the sick, for they were nailed to the cross. His feet could no longer take Him to minister God's mercy to those in need, because they were nailed to the cross. However, there was one thing He still could do. He could pray. Jesus continued His ministry of prayer for others even while hanging on the cross. Even in His dying hours He was carrying out the instruction He had given in the Sermon on the Mount: "I say unto you, Love your enemies, bless them that curse you, do good to them that hate you, and pray for them which despitefully use you, and persecute you" (Matthew 5:44). With His dying breath Christ gave us a powerful example of how we are to treat those who curse us, hate us, despitefully use us, and persecute us.

Christ's example in this first saying from the cross contains a lesson for us. We may find ourselves limited in what we can do for the Lord or others because of some infirmity or other that limits us physically. However, we can always pray. The truth is that prayer is the most powerful force on earth. In fact, we may accomplish more through our prayers than we ever could by our active labor. Ellen White confirmed this when she wrote: "Through much prayer you must labor for souls, for this is the *only method* by which you can reach hearts. It is not your work, but the work of Christ who is by your side, that impresses hearts" (*Evangelism,* p. 342; emphasis added).

The book of Acts tells us that Christ's prayer was extremely effective. Following Peter's sermon on the

Day of Pentecost, three thousand people were baptized. Later, we read of five thousand being converted (see Acts 4). We must never stop praying for our friends and loved ones who have fallen away from Christ or who have never accepted Him as their personal Savior.

Isaiah 53 contains ten prophetic statements about the Messiah's suffering. He would be despised and rejected of men, a man of sorrows and acquainted with grief. He would be wounded, bruised, chastised; would go unresisting to the slaughter; be dumb before the shearers; suffer at the hands of men; and be bruised by the Lord. He would pour out His soul unto death, be buried in a rich man's tomb, be numbered with transgressors, and make intercession for them. Christ's first saying while He was on the cross fulfilled this last prophecy—that He would "make intercession for transgressors." The Jesus hanging on the cross was truly the Messiah foretold in the Old Testament.

The cross led to the tomb, which caused great fear and discouragement in the hearts of the disciples. The cross also led His persecutors—along with Satan and his evil host—to rejoice, thinking this was the end of Jesus of Nazareth. Little did they know that what appeared to be the end and a great defeat was actually a great victory. We should learn the lesson that events that appear to us to be a great defeat may be regarded by God to be a great victory.

On the third day after His crucifixion, the great tombstone was rolled away and Christ was raised from the dead by the Spirit of God. Concerning Christ's resurrection, Paul wrote that He was "declared to be the Son of God with power, according to the spirit of holiness, by the resurrection from the dead" (Romans 1:4). Christ's release from the tomb was the divine declaration that He is the Messiah and Savior He claimed to be. If you haven't accepted Him as your Savior, don't let another day go by without giving your life to Christ.

Discussion Questions

1. **What was the first saying of Christ on the cross?** _____

2. **What primary truth about God was revealed in Christ's first saying on the cross?** _____
_____

3. **What example did Christ give us in this prayer regarding our attitude toward those who mistreat us?** _____

4. **Was Christ's prayer effective? Why?** _____

5. **What Old Testament prophecy was Christ fulfilling with this first saying from the cross?** ___
_____

6. **Why should we not become discouraged when we or God's work suffers what seems to be a defeat?** _____

Prayer Focus
Pray for:

- **God to fill you with the Holy Spirit.**
- **God to give you the desire to be like Christ in praying for others.**
- **Those on your prayer list.**

Day 18

The First Saying of Christ on the Cross—Part 2

In today's devotional we will once again consider Christ's first saying on the cross: "Father, forgive them; for they know not what they do" (Luke 23:34).

Throughout Christ's ministry He forgave men and women for their sins. He had the authority to do that because He was God in the flesh. Jesus explicitly said this: "The Son of man hath power on earth to forgive sins" (Matthew 9:6). According to the Bible, if human beings were to claim to have the authority to forgive sins, they would be blaspheming. Note what the scribes and Pharisees said of Jesus when He forgave a bedridden man sick with palsy. Luke writes that when Jesus saw their faith, "he said unto him, Man, thy sins are forgiven thee. And the scribes and the Pharisees began to reason, saying, Who is this which speaketh blasphemies? Who can forgive sins, but God alone?" (Luke 5:20, 21).

However, when Jesus hung on the cross, instead of forgiving those who were crucifying Him, He asked His Father to forgive them. What had changed? Well, Jesus was "lifted up from the earth" (John 12:32). He hung on the cross as our representative and substitute. He was no longer in a place of authority. If He was to be our substitute, He must identify with us completely. He was dying in our stead that we might be forgiven and have eternal life.

Here once again we see Christ giving us an amazing example of forgiveness. In the Sermon on the Mount He told us to pray for and to forgive those who persecute us. We must never harbor ill feelings or anger toward anyone, no matter what they have done to us. If we do, we give Satan a foothold in our life. Paul wrote, "Be ye angry, and sin not: let not the sun go down upon your wrath: neither give place to the devil" (Ephesians 4:26, 27). If we cherish anger and allow it to keep us from forgiving those who have harmed us, we will be destroyed spiritually, emotionally, and even physically. Such an attitude will harm others and even threaten our eternal destiny. "Follow peace with all men, and holiness, without which no man shall see the Lord: looking diligently lest any man fail of the grace of God; lest any root of bitterness springing up trouble you, and thereby many be defiled" (Hebrews 12:14, 15).

We also find in Christ's first statement from the cross the statement "they know not what they do." Here we see how truly blind the human heart is. Those for whom Christ prayed had no idea of what a terrible sin they were committing. They didn't know that they were crucifying the Son of God, the Messiah, the One who came to save them, the most loving Person who ever walked this earth. They should have known. They had evidence in the many Old Testament prophecies about the Messiah that Jesus had fulfilled. Many saw and even more heard of His miracles of healing the sick, casting out devils, and even raising the dead. His teachings of love were heard day after day for three and a half years. Yet, in spite of all this evidence, they cried out, "Crucify Him!"

God has made provision for sins of ignorance. The Old Testament Levitical law allowed for forgiveness of sins that people committed unknowingly. It is as important that these sins of ignorance be forgiven as it is to have obtained forgiveness for our known sins. Concerning the importance of complete forgiveness of all sins, known and unknown, David prayed, "Who

can understand his errors? cleanse thou me from secret faults" (Psalm 19:12).

The tragedy of the cross repeats itself today. Men and women still reject the great salvation God is offering all humanity. Spiritual blindness covers their eyes. We also must pray as Christ did that God would forgive them and save them, for Christ's first saying from the cross clearly reveals the salvation God offers to even the vilest of sinners: "As Moses lifted up the serpent in the wilderness, even so must the Son of man be lifted up: that whosoever believeth in him should not perish, but have eternal life. For God so loved the world, that he gave his only begotten Son, that whosoever believeth in him should not perish, but have everlasting life. For God sent not his Son into the world to condemn the world; but that the world through him might be saved" (John 3:14–17).

Discussion Questions

1. Why was Jesus able to forgive sins when He was here on earth?

2. Why did Jesus ask the Father to forgive His persecutors when He was on the cross?

3. Why is it important that we forgive those who have wronged us?

4. Is it important that we ask for forgiveness of sins of ignorance? Why?

5. In your opinion, why do men and women reject Christ today?

6. How should we relate to people who reject Christ?

Prayer Focus
Pray for:

- God to fill you with the Holy Spirit.
- God to give you a heart to forgive all who have wronged you.
- Those on your prayer list.

The Second Saying of Christ on the Cross—Part 1

Jesus was crucified between two thieves. One of them "railed on him, saying, If thou be Christ, save thyself and us" (Luke 23:39). The other, turning his head to Jesus as best he could, asked, "Lord, remember me when thou comest into thy kingdom. And Jesus said unto him, Verily I say unto thee, Today shalt thou be with me in paradise" (Luke 23:42, 43).

It was in God's divine providence that Jesus was crucified between two thieves. Scripture declares that God foreordains all things, "for of a truth against thy holy child Jesus, whom thou hast anointed, both Herod, and Pontius Pilate, with the Gentiles, and the people of Israel, were gathered together, for to do whatsoever thy hand and thy counsel determined before to be done" (Acts 4:27, 28). God's Word had said that Christ would be "numbered with the transgressors" (Isaiah 53:12). It is important that we never forget that all that God has ordained will come to pass. "There are many devices in a man's heart; nevertheless the counsel of the LORD, that shall stand" (Proverbs 19:21). Knowledge of God's sovereignty should give every Christian assurance that God is in control no matter how chaotic events become or how hopeless a situation appears.

Some mistakenly use this second statement of Christ to teach that man goes to heaven or hell at death. However, the Bible clearly teaches that God's people receive their reward at Christ's second coming: "For as in Adam all die, even so in Christ shall all be made alive. But every man in his own order: Christ the firstfruits; afterward they that are Christ's at his coming" (1 Corinthians 15:22, 23). Jesus was assuring the repentant thief at that moment, on that day, that he would be with Christ in His future kingdom of glory.

This second statement of Christ clearly reveals God's grace toward the sinner. This thief had done nothing to earn his salvation. He was a convicted thief; just a few moments before, he had confessed that to the other thief. However, at the moment he yielded to the conviction brought by the Holy Spirit that the man being crucified next to him was not only innocent, but was the Christ, he simply put his faith in Christ, asking Him to save him in His kingdom. Truly, salvation is by faith; "for by grace are ye saved through faith; and that not of yourselves: it is the gift of God: Not of works, lest any man should boast" (Ephesians 2:8, 9).

What an amazing work of grace we see here! This thief had walked with Christ, who was carrying His cross in the streets, and he had seen Christ fall under the weight of the cross. He was seeing Christ at the time when He was disgraced and at His weakest. He heard the onlookers shout hatefully against Christ. He even saw Christ's disciples flee in fear, having lost hope that Jesus was the Messiah.

This scene that featured a cross differed completely from the view everyone had of the Messiah. Even John the Baptist questioned whether Jesus was truly the Messiah, since He wasn't doing what John believed the Messiah would do. Even the thief that believed in Jesus had earlier joined the other thief in mocking Jesus, "In the same way the rebels who were crucified with him also heaped insults on him (Matthew 27:44, NIV). Yet, in spite of all the evidence against Jesus' being the Messiah, and despite the other thief's mocking of Jesus, in a moment during which he experienced the active impact of God's grace on his heart by the power of the Holy Spirit, this thief yielded to that convicting power and

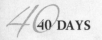

chose to believe in Jesus as the Savior and Messiah.

Truly, grace is amazing!

This thief's condition before accepting Christ is representative of all humanity. "As it is written, There is none righteous, no, not one: There is none that understandeth, there is none that seeketh after God. They are all gone out of the way, they are together become unprofitable; there is none that doeth good, no, not one. . . . For all have sinned, and come short of the glory of God" (Romans 3:10–12, 23).

This thief's recognition of his sinfulness and his despairing of anything he could do to save himself portray the first steps all people must take to be saved. Once sinners, by the Holy Spirit's convicting power, recognize their true condition before God, they must at once reach out to Christ as this thief did and trust Jesus to save them and reserve a place for them in God's kingdom.

Discussion Questions

1. **Why was Christ crucified between two thieves?** _____

   _____

2. **What assurance does God's sovereignty give you?** _____

   _____

3. **How many of the thieves mocked Jesus?** _____

4. **Why do you think so many rejected Jesus as the Messiah?** _____

   _____

5. **Why did one thief change his mind about Jesus and accept Him as his Savior?** _____

   _____

6. **What promise did Jesus make to the thief who believed in Him?** _____

   _____

7. **In what way is the thief who accepted Christ representative of all humanity?** _____

8. **What is the first step toward receiving salvation?** _____

Prayer Focus

Pray for:

- God to fill you with the Holy Spirit.
- God to continue to convict you to yield your life to Jesus every day.
- Those on your prayer list.

Day 20

The Second Saying of Christ on the Cross—Part 2

Jesus was crucified between two thieves. The following verses acquaint us with the verbal exchange between the two thieves: "One of the malefactors which were hanged railed on him, saying, If thou be Christ, save thyself and us. But the other answering rebuked him, saying, Dost not thou fear God, seeing thou art in the same condemnation? And we indeed justly; for we receive the due reward of our deeds: but this man hath done nothing amiss" (Luke 23:39–41).

Here we see the amazing insight that was given to the thief who recognized Jesus for who He was in spite of His hanging on a cross. This thief rebuked the other thief for not fearing God. He was convicted that a time would come when sinners would be judged by a holy God. He recognized his own sinfulness and that he was justly condemned. He also recognized Jesus' innocence.

We also see that this thief recognized Jesus' divinity, in that he addressed Jesus as Lord and accepted Him as his Savior when he asked Jesus to remember him. His words also reveal that he recognized Jesus' royalty—he asked Jesus to remember him when He came into His "kingdom" (verse 42). And his words here reveal that he knew that Jesus' kingdom of glory was to be set up sometime in the future. As this thief hung on the cross next to Jesus, he accepted the hope that someday Jesus would return and establish His kingdom, and he wanted to have a part in that kingdom.

Amazing grace! The enlightening grace of the Holy Spirit had illuminated the mind of this dying thief, and he accepted Christ as his Savior and received the assurance that he would be with Christ in His kingdom. Jesus' restraint and refusal to respond to the crowd by returning their mocking and reproaches is a powerful testimony of Jesus' love—as is His ignoring the insults that the priests cast on Him. Instead, Jesus responded to the prayer of a repentant, believing, dying thief. In this, Jesus was once again fulfilling His mission. He said, "If any man hear my words, and believe not, I judge him not: for I came not to judge the world, but to save the world" (John 12:47). Even during His dying hours Jesus was still ministering love, hope, and salvation.

In spite of Jesus' struggle with the powers of darkness when He felt the terrible weight of the sins of His people and experienced terrible physical and mental anguish, He still responded to the cry of a repentant sinner. Words cannot describe the love of God toward His people and the depth of His desire to save them. Surely, Micah was right when he said that God "delights in mercy" (Micah 7:18, NKJV). God's great desire is to show mercy to sinners and to save us from our sins.

The words of assurance that Jesus spoke to the thief clearly reveal that there is never an inappropriate or unacceptable time to reach out to Jesus for forgiveness and to receive the assurance of eternal life. We must never let anything keep us away from bringing our sins to Jesus, where we will receive forgiveness and the assurance of being in His kingdom, "for he saith, I have heard thee in a time accepted, and in the day of salvation have I succoured thee: behold, now is the accepted time; behold, now is the day of salvation" (2 Corinthians 6:2).

Christ's words to the thief also assure us that there truly is a paradise, or a kingdom of glory, where we

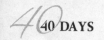

will be with Christ. John the revelator wrote of this, saying, "He that hath an ear, let him hear what the Spirit saith unto the churches; To him that overcometh will I give to eat of the tree of life, which is in the midst of the paradise of God" (Revelation 2:7).

The purpose of the plan of salvation is to restore man back to a close, intimate fellowship with Jesus. "God is faithful, by whom ye were called unto the fellowship of his Son Jesus Christ our Lord" (1 Corinthians 1:9). This fellowship begins when we accept Jesus as our Savior. Paul describes what happens when Jesus returns and confirms that our fellowship with Jesus

will last forever in His kingdom of glory: "The Lord himself shall descend from heaven with a shout, with the voice of the archangel, and with the trump of God: and the dead in Christ shall rise first: Then we which are alive and remain shall be caught up together with them in the clouds, to meet the Lord in the air: and so shall we ever be with the Lord" (1 Thessalonians 4:16, 17). Our greatest joy in heaven will be our fellowship with our Lord. "Thou wilt [show] me the path of life: in thy presence is [fullness] of joy; at thy right hand there are pleasures for evermore" (Psalm 16:11).

Discussion Questions

1. **What statements did the thief make that indicate he was enlightened by the Holy Spirit and accepted those truths?** _____

2. **What did this saved thief recognize about Jesus that the other thief did not?** _____

_____

3. **What did Jesus' reply to this thief reveal about Jesus?** _____

_____

4. **What did Jesus' words reveal about the reality of a heavenly paradise?** _____

_____

5. **What is the primary purpose of the plan of salvation as regards humanity?** _____

_____

Prayer Focus

Pray for:

- **God to fill you with the Holy Spirit.**
- **God to reveal to you how truly loving and compassionate He is toward you.**
- **Those on your prayer list.**

Day 21

The Third Saying of Christ on the Cross—Part 1

The third saying of Christ on the cross is found in John 19:25–27, "Now there stood by the cross of Jesus his mother, and his mother's sister, Mary the wife of Cleophas, and Mary Magdalene. When Jesus therefore saw his mother, and the disciple standing by, whom he loved, he saith unto his mother, Woman, behold thy son! Then saith he to the disciple, Behold thy mother! And from that hour that disciple took her unto his own home."

When Mary was a young woman, God called her to be the mother of Jesus. Being chosen by God to be the mother of the Messiah was the greatest honor ever given to a human being. However, with that honor also came great trials and heartache. God warned Mary of this through an elderly man named Simeon. When Jesus was eight days old, Joseph and Mary brought Him to the temple to be circumcised and dedicated to God. While they were there, God revealed to Simeon that Jesus was the Messiah, and Simeon told Mary, "Behold, this child is set for the fall and rising again of many in Israel; and for a sign which shall be spoken against; (Yea, a sword shall pierce through thy own soul also,) that the thoughts of many hearts may be revealed" (Luke 2:34, 35).

Being Jesus' mother brought great joy to Mary, but her heart was filled with great sorrow when she beheld her Son beaten, bloodied, crucified, and dying on the cross. This fulfilled Simeon's prophecy that a sword would pierce through her own soul.

We also see a mother's love revealed at the cross. Christ's disciples had deserted Him, and His nation was rejecting Him and calling for His death. Yet, His mother stood by Him as He hung on the cross.

All Christians experience something similar. They know great joy when Christ comes into their life and they are born again. The forgiveness of sin and the assurance of eternal life are wonderful. However, they soon discover that, as the apostle Paul put it, "we must through much tribulation enter into the kingdom of God" (Acts 14:22). I'm sure Mary didn't understand all the reasons God had for allowing her Son to suffer such terrible things. However, three days later, when He was resurrected, she realized that He had gained a great victory over sin and death.

So it is with all Christians. Many things happen in their lives that they don't understand. At such times they have to trust God's promises, such as "we know that all things work together for good to them that love God, to them who are the called according to his purpose" (Romans 8:28), and "count it all joy when ye fall into divers temptations; knowing this, that the trying of your faith worketh patience. But let patience have her perfect work, that ye may be perfect and entire, wanting nothing" (James 1:2–4).

Christ's words in this third saying from the cross also reveal His love for and honor of His mother. Even when He was on the cross, He kept God's command to "honour thy father and thy mother" (Exodus 20:12).

Honoring our parents goes beyond simple obedience to their instruction. Honoring them means loving them, expressing our gratitude to them, and respecting them. This command applies to every son and daughter, whether they are children living at home or adults out on their own.

Jesus fulfilled God's instruction that we are to "hearken unto thy father that begat thee, and despise not thy mother when she is old" (Proverbs 23:22). So

we are to show respect whether we consider our parents to be good or bad. Paul wrote, "Children, obey your parents in the Lord: for this is right. Honour thy father and mother; which is the first commandment with promise; That it may be well with thee, and thou mayest live long on the earth. And, ye fathers, provoke not your children to wrath: but bring them up in the nurture and admonition of the Lord" (Ephesians 6:1–4). We are to honor them both when they are still living and when they have passed away.

In this, Jesus' third saying on the cross, we see Him addressing His mother as "woman." This was a respectful term of address. He held His mother is great esteem—so much so that even at the most difficult time in His life, when He hung on the cross, He was concerned enough about her future to provide for her care.

Discussion Questions

1. How do you think Mary felt when she was told she was to give birth to Jesus? _____

    _____

2. What did Simeon mean when he told Mary that her soul would be pierced with a sword? ___

    _____

3. What do you think motivated Mary to stay by the cross as Jesus hung there dying? _____

    _____

4. What does every Christian go through that is similar to what Mary experienced after giving birth to Jesus? _____

5. Will Christians always understand why God allows them to go through difficult trials? ____

    _____

6. How did Christ reveal His honor for His mother, Mary? _____

    _____

7. What attitude should all Christians have regarding their parents, whether they've been good or bad parents, and whether they are still living or are deceased? _____

    _____

Prayer Focus
Pray for:

- God to fill you with the Holy Spirit.
- God to reveal to you how He wants you to honor your parents.
- God to give you the faith to trust Him during difficult times.
- Those on your prayer list.

Day 22

The Third Saying of Christ on the Cross—Part 2

Christ's third saying on the cross expressed His loving concern for His mother: "Now there stood by the cross of Jesus his mother, and his mother's sister, Mary the wife of Cleophas, and Mary Magdalene. When Jesus therefore saw his mother, and the disciple standing by, whom he loved, he saith unto his mother, Woman, behold thy son! Then saith he to the disciple, Behold thy mother! And from that hour that disciple took her unto his own home" (John 19:25–27).

Here we see that John stood by Jesus during His most trying hour. Other than the severing of His relationship with His Father due to our sin, His disciples' forsaking Him brought Jesus the most pain He experienced while here on earth. Jesus had previously warned them that they would be offended, scandalized, and ashamed because of Him. He said, "All ye shall be offended because of me this night: for it is written, I will smite the shepherd, and the sheep of the flock shall be scattered abroad" (Matthew 26:31). Only one of the eleven stayed with Christ—though at a distance—while He was on the cross.

We might say, "I would have been faithful to Jesus during His trial and crucifixion." However, we don't differ much from those disciples. We, too, as disciples of Christ have at times wandered away from Him during difficult times in our life. We may have become angry at God for letting us face some crisis. We may have stopped attending church because of something someone said to us. Or at some time we may have hesitated to speak up for Christ because we were afraid of what others would think of us. Or perhaps we stopped returning a faithful tithe to God because we didn't trust Him to bless us as He promised.

It's important we notice how Christ treated the disciples following His resurrection. He didn't rebuke them, but He gave them the honor and privilege of taking the gospel of Jesus Christ to the world. And the gates of the New Jerusalem are named for them. From their failure to stand by Jesus they learned the truth of His saying that he who is forgiven the most loves the most. So it will be with us. When we have let our Savior down by some willful action and then repent and return to Christ and see that He truly forgives us and honors us again with the privilege of serving Him, we will love Him even more.

This third saying also reveals Christ's wisdom. John was the most loving of all the disciples, and he understood Christ's love better than did the other disciples. In addition, John and Mary had a special bond in that they both loved Jesus very deeply. They had a special blessed spiritual fellowship together. Christians who truly love Jesus will want to fellowship with fellow believers. There will be a deep spiritual bond between them. Malachi recognized this when he wrote, "They that feared the LORD spake often one to another: and the LORD hearkened, and heard it, and a book of remembrance was written before him for them that feared the LORD, and that thought upon his name" (Malachi 3:16).

In asking John to care for His mother, Mary, Jesus set an important example for us. We are not to neglect our responsibility to our family relationships. We mustn't allow even spiritual responsibilities to cause us to neglect our families. On the other hand, of course, we mustn't allow our family responsibilities to become an excuse for ignoring our moral responsibilities. If we ask God, He will lead us in this important area of relationships in our life.

I'm amazed at how loving, caring, and giving Christ was. Even while being nailed to the cross, enduring the mocking of onlookers, bleeding, and dying an awful death, He not only prays that those who are crucifying Him be forgiven, but He also ministers to a man who is reaching out to Him for salvation, He considers His mother's future needs, and He gives John the precious responsibility of caring for His mother.

Christ has not changed. He is the same yesterday, today, and forever. He still intercedes for us, ministers to bring salvation to us, and cares deeply for each of us. He who in His dying hour made provision for His mother's care will also make provision for the needs we have today, whether they be physical, emotional, or spiritual.

Discussion Questions

1. **Which of the twelve disciples remained faithful to Him during His most trying hour?** _____
    _____

2. **Personally reflect on a time when you chose to turn from Christ during a trying time in your life. How did Christ relate to you when you returned to Him?** _____
    _____

3. **How did you feel toward Christ when you had failed Him and then returned to Him and He honored you again with the privilege of serving Him?** _____
    _____

4. **Why was it a wise decision for Jesus to ask John to care for His mother?** _____
    _____

5. **What example did Jesus give us concerning our families when He asked John to care for Mary?**
    _____

6. **What assurance does Jesus' making provision for His mother's care give us?**_____
    _____

Prayer Focus
Pray for:

- ● **God to fill you with the Holy Spirit.**
- ● **God to give you the faith to believe He will provide for you at all times.**
- ● **Those on your prayer list.**

The Fourth Saying of Christ on the Cross—Part 1

The fourth saying of Christ on the cross is quoted in the following text: "And about the ninth hour Jesus cried with a loud voice, saying, Eli, Eli, lama sabachthani? that is to say, My God, my God, why hast thou forsaken me?" (Matthew 27:46). Jesus had been with the Father from eternity past: "In the beginning was the Word, and the Word was with God, and the Word was God. The same was in the beginning with God" (John 1:1, 2). During all that time He had an intimate, loving relationship with the Father. That was true also of the time He walked on earth. He said, "Believest thou not that I am in the Father, and the Father in me? the words that I speak unto you I speak not of myself: but the Father that dwelleth in me, he doeth the works" (John 14:10). Jesus often spent entire nights in prayer with His Father. In fact, He taught that "I and my Father are one" (John 10:30).

However, when Christ allowed our sins to be placed on Himself on the cross, they severed the intimate relationship Christ had with His Father. This was the bitterest experience Christ had while on earth. He felt the separation and condemnation that all sinners will feel who haven't accepted Christ as their Savior. This shows how great is the love Christ has for us—in order that we can be saved, He was willing to suffer the damnable separation from God that sinners will feel when they realize they are lost.

Jesus' fourth saying while He was on the cross reveals the true character of sin and God's inflexible attitude toward it. Sin separates humans from God. Isaiah said it more poetically: "Your iniquities have separated between you and your God, and your sins have hid his face from you, that he will not hear" (Isaiah 59:2).

On the cross, sin separated Christ from His Father. Again, Isaiah said it so well: "Surely he hath borne our griefs, and carried our sorrows: yet we did esteem him stricken, smitten of God, and afflicted. But he was wounded for our transgressions, he was bruised for our iniquities: the chastisement of our peace was upon him; and with his stripes we are healed. All we like sheep have gone astray; we have turned every one to his own way; and the LORD hath laid on him the iniquity of us all" (Isaiah 53:4–6).

Sin separates sinners from God eternally. Paul said that they "shall be punished with everlasting destruction from the presence of the Lord, and from the glory of his power" (2 Thessalonians 1:9). When Christ cried out, "My God, my God, why hast thou forsaken me," He could not see beyond the tomb. He was experiencing the absolute separation from God all sinners will suffer when the dictates of the final judgment are carried out. But this fourth saying of Jesus while He was on the cross reveals that He loves sinners even more than He loved Himself. He was willing to sacrifice Himself completely for us.

Here we also learn of God's absolute holiness and inflexible justice. God is holy, and holiness is repulsed by sin. God is just, and His justice demands punishment for sin. Christ, the Sinless One, the Righteous One, the Holy One, was "made . . . to be sin for us, who knew no sin; that we might be made the righteousness of God in him" (2 Corinthians 5:21). If God was to deal righteously and justly with the sins of His people, someone must bear them. Since Jesus had agreed to take on Himself the responsibility for those sins, they had to be poured out on Him as He hung on the cross.

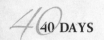

In this saying, we see the destiny of all those who choose not to accept Christ's substitutionary death on their behalf. Christ's words foretell their eternal death—their final, complete, and eternal separation from God. "He that believeth on the Son hath everlasting life: and he that believeth not the Son shall not see life; but the wrath of God abideth on him" (John 3:36).

It is sad, but true. Jesus Christ has made salvation, eternal fellowship with God, eternal life, available to all. Yet many will choose not to accept the wonderful gift His bearing the cross has enabled Him to give them. To those who accept Him as their Savior, Jesus has given this wonderful promise: "This is the record, that God hath given to us eternal life, and this life is in his Son. He that hath the Son hath life; and he that hath not the Son of God hath not life. These things have I written unto you that believe on the name of the Son of God; that ye may know that ye have eternal life, and that ye may believe on the name of the Son of God" (1 John 5:11–13).

Discussion Questions

1. **How long had Christ been with the Father before He came to planet Earth?** _____

2. **How would you describe Christ's relationship with the Father?** _____

3. **What does Christ's cry, "My God, my God, why hast thou forsaken me?" indicate about His relationship with the Father at the moment He asked that question while on the cross?** _____

4. **What does this fourth saying of Christ indicate about God's attitude toward sin?** _____

5. **What does this fourth saying of Christ teach us about God's character?** _____

6. **What does this fourth saying of Christ reveal about the destiny of those who choose not to accept Him?** _____

7. **What is the destiny of all who accept Christ as their Savior?** _____

Prayer Focus
Pray for:

- **God to fill you with the Holy Spirit.**
- **God to enable you to realize the sacrifice Christ made for you on the cross.**
- **Those on your prayer list.**

Day 24

The Fourth Saying of Christ on the Cross—Part 2

The fourth saying of Christ on the cross, "Eli, Eli, lama sabachthani? that is to say, My God, my God, why hast thou forsaken me?" (Matthew 27:46), reveals many truths about God. In this statement we learn that there is a limit to God's mercy. We see this illustrated by how, in Old Testament times, God dealt with the sins of His people and their refusal to respond to what He said to them. They reached a point of no return—a point beyond which there was no way to avert God's judgments on them.

They refused to hearken, and pulled away the shoulder, and stopped their ears, that they should not hear. Yea, they made their hearts as an adamant stone, lest they should hear the law, and the words which the Lord of hosts hath sent in his spirit by the former prophets: therefore came a great wrath from the Lord of hosts. Therefore it is come to pass, that as he cried, and they would not hear; so they cried, and I would not hear, saith the Lord of hosts: But I scattered them with a whirlwind among all the nations whom they knew not. Thus the land was desolate after them, that no man passed through nor returned: for they laid the pleasant land desolate (Zechariah 7:11–14).

So also, there is a limit to God's mercy on a sinful world. A great judgment day is coming for every sinner. John pictured it this way:

I saw a great white throne, and him that sat on it, from whose face the earth and the heaven fled away; and there was found no place for them. And I saw the dead, small and great, stand before God; and the books were opened: and another book was opened, which is the book of life: and the dead were judged out of those things which were written in the books, according to their works. And the sea gave up the dead which were in it; and death and hell delivered up the dead which were in them: and they were judged every man according to their works. And death and hell were cast into the lake of fire. This is the second death. And whosoever was not found written in the book of life was cast into the lake of fire (Revelation 20:11–15).

In Christ's cry of "My God, My God, why hast thou forsaken me?" we see that Christ was suffering the curse that sin brings on all sinners. Paul writes of this curse: "Christ hath redeemed us from the curse of the law, being made a curse for us: for it is written, Cursed is every one that hangeth on a tree" (Galatians 3:13).

We also find in Christ's agonizing cry the explanation of His words in the Garden of Gethsemane: "My soul is exceeding sorrowful, even unto death" (Matthew 26:38). The expression "exceeding sorrowful" means "I'm overwhelmed with sorrow." Christ was feeling deep within Himself the anticipation of suffering God's wrath. It seemed too overwhelming; too terrible to endure. Because of this foretaste sense of the sins of His people being placed on Him and His separation from the Father, He fell on His face and earnestly prayed, "O my Father, if it be possible, let this cup pass from me: nevertheless not as I will, but as thou wilt" (verse 39).

In truth, the victory of the cross was actually gained

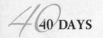

in the garden. Once Christ made the decision to yield to the Father's will, the cross was inevitable—and the victory was sure. So it is many times with the Christian. The victory over sin is gained in one's quiet time with God. Once the surrender is made in prayer, the victory will become a reality when the temptation comes.

In Christ's words "My God, My God, why hast thou forsaken me?" we see undisputable evidence of God's love for His people: "Greater love hath no man than this, that a man lay down his life for his friends" (John 15:13). The Sinless One allowed our sins to so engulf Him that they severed the relationship He had enjoyed with His Father. Christ allowed Himself to experience the curse—God's forsaking of sin and those who choose to remain in it.

Amazing love!

Discussion Questions

1. **What is the meaning of the statement "God's mercy has a limit"?** _____

   _____

2. **What is the implication for the world of the fact that God's mercy is limited?** _____

   _____

3. **What was Christ feeling in the Garden of Gethsemane that caused Him to ask the Father to take the "cup" from Him?** _____

4. **What important issue did Christ settle in the garden?** _____

   _____

5. **Explain the role of prayer in your life.** _____

   _____

6. **What amazing truth about God is revealed in the fourth saying of Christ on the cross?** _____

   _____

Prayer Focus

Pray for:

- **God to fill you with the Holy Spirit.**
- **God to give you a greater understanding of His love for you as revealed at the cross.**
- **Those on your prayer list.**

Day 25

The Fifth Saying of Christ on the Cross—Part 1

In today's devotional we will consider Christ's fifth saying on the cross. It is found in John 19:28, 29: "After this, Jesus knowing that all things were now accomplished, that the scripture might be fulfilled, saith, I thirst. Now there was set a vessel full of vinegar: and they filled a sponge with vinegar, and put it upon hyssop, and put it to his mouth."

The Old Testament foretold many things that the Messiah would experience. This was one of them. Psalm 69:21 says, "They gave me [the Messiah] also gall for my meat; and in my thirst they gave me vinegar to drink." All those who doubt that Jesus was who He claimed to be are ignorant of the Old Testament scripture. The Old Testament contains the prophecy that He would be betrayed by a "familiar friend": "Yea, mine own familiar friend, in whom I trusted, which did eat of my bread, hath lifted up his heel against me" (Psalm 41:9). Isaiah 53 lists many things Christ would experience. He would be silent before His accusers (verse 7). He would be numbered with the transgressors, which was fulfilled when Jesus was crucified between two convicted thieves (verse 12). He would pray for His accusers (ibid.). He would be buried in a rich man's tomb (verse 9). Not one bone would be broken (Psalm 34:20).

Scripture even foretold the manner in which He would die—crucifixion: "Dogs have compassed me: the assembly of the wicked have enclosed me: they pierced my hands and my feet" (Psalm 22:16). And these are just some of the Old Testament's prophecies; many more could be listed. So, God's Word is clear. Jesus was truly the Christ, the Messiah whom Israel had longed for over the centuries.

These prophetic statements that were clearly fulfilled by Jesus Christ are also evidence that the book known as the Bible is God's inspired Word. That Jesus believed this to be true is apparent in that He applied them to Himself. He said, "Search the scriptures; for in them ye think ye have eternal life: and they are they which testify of me" (John 5:39). And Paul wrote, "All scripture is given by inspiration of God, and is profitable for doctrine, for reproof, for correction, for instruction in righteousness: That the man of God may be perfect, thoroughly furnished unto all good works" (2 Timothy 3:16, 17).

Jesus' statement "I thirst" reveals His humanity. He was both fully God and fully man. When God "the Word became flesh" in the person of Jesus Christ (John 1:1–3, 14), He laid aside His divinity because He was to be our substitute in all things. "Let this mind be in you, which was also in Christ Jesus: who, being in the form of God, thought it not robbery to be equal with God: But made himself of no reputation, and took upon him the form of a servant, and was made in the likeness of men: And being found in fashion as a man, he humbled himself, and became obedient unto death, even the death of the cross" (Philippians 2:5–8).

Old Testament Scripture had foretold this as well. The Messiah would be of the "seed" of a woman (Genesis 3:15); He would be a prophet like Moses (Deuteronomy 18:18); He would be a descendant of David (2 Samuel 7:12, 13), and He would be a "man" of sorrows (Isaiah 53:3).

Christ's statement "I thirst" expresses the physical suffering He was experiencing. In the preceding hours He didn't complain or plead for mercy even though He

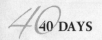

had been betrayed, falsely accused, beaten, mocked, and nailed to the cross.

His statement also expresses what Psalm 42:1–3 says, "As the hart panteth after the water brooks, so panteth my soul after thee, O God. My soul thirsteth for God, for the living God: when shall I come and appear before God? My tears have been my meat day and night, while they continually say unto me, Where is thy God?" Jesus had just experienced the severing of His relationship with His Father because of our sins. His words "I thirst" express the agony of soul with which He longed for the relationship with His Father that now seemed to have been taken from Him.

Do you hunger and thirst for a closer relationship with God? Do you long for intimacy with Him? Do you long to walk with God every day as Enoch did? Is it your heart's desire to spend eternity with Him? Jesus promised that such thirsting after God will be satisfied: "Blessed are they which do hunger and thirst after righteousness: for they shall be filled" (Matthew 5:6).

Discussion Questions

1. **List some of the Old Testament prophecies that prove Jesus was the long looked-for Messiah.**

   _____

2. **What does Christ's statement "I thirst" reveal about His humanity?** _____

   _____

3. **What does Christ's statement "I thirst" reveal about His spiritual desires?** _____

   _____

4. **What does it mean to thirst for God?** _____

Prayer Focus

Pray for:

- **God to fill you with the Holy Spirit.**
- **God to give you a thirst for a closer relationship with Himself.**
- **Those on your prayer list.**

Day 26

The Fifth Saying of Christ on the Cross—Part 2

The fifth saying of Christ on the cross, "I thirst," shows that Christ understood Scripture and wanted to fulfill its prophecies. "After this, Jesus knowing that all things were now accomplished, that the scripture might be fulfilled, saith, I thirst" (John 19:28). Christ knew the prophetic declaration the psalmist wrote, "They gave me also gall for my meat; and in my thirst they gave me vinegar to drink" (Psalm 69:21).

Christ's mind was clear, and He didn't want to take anything to cloud His thinking. He knew what Scripture taught about Himself, and He was determined to fulfill every detail. During His entire life He yielded to the will of His Father: "Jesus saith unto them, My meat is to do the will of him that sent me, and to finish his work" (John 4:34). The psalmist had prophesied this would be the desire of the Messiah: "Then said I, Lo, I come: in the volume of the book it is written of me, I delight to do thy will, O my God: yea, thy law is within my heart" (Psalm 40:7, 8). Jesus constantly yielded to the will of His Father.

Can the same be said of each of us? Is it our one desire to yield to God's will as revealed in Scripture? This will be the experience of those who are ready for Christ's return; they will be just like Jesus. John pointed this out: "Beloved, now are we the sons of God, and it doth not yet appear what we shall be: but we know that, when he shall appear, we shall be like him; for we shall see him as he is" (1 John 3:2). May our desire be like that of the psalmist when he wrote, "Teach me, O LORD, the way of thy statutes; and I shall keep it unto the end. Give me understanding, and I shall keep thy law; yea, I shall observe it with my whole heart. Make me to go in the path of thy commandments; for therein do I delight. Incline my heart unto thy testimonies, and not to covetousness" (Psalm 119:33–36).

Those who are like Jesus when He returns will have the same desire Jesus has to faithfully obey God. May our great desire be "Keep back thy servant also from presumptuous sins; let them not have dominion over me: then shall I be upright, and I shall be innocent from the great transgression. Let the words of my mouth, and the meditation of my heart, be acceptable in thy sight, O LORD, my strength, and my redeemer" (Psalm 19:13, 14).

In this fifth statement of Christ we see another aspect of His submission to His Father's will. Jesus is the Creator of all things: "For by him were all things created, that are in heaven, and that are in earth, visible and invisible, whether they be thrones, or dominions, or principalities, or powers: all things were created by him, and for him: And he is before all things, and by him all things consist" (Colossians 1:16, 17). Christ created every stream, lake, and ocean, so He could have provided for Himself any amount of water to quench His thirst. Yet He chose to die as our Substitute and didn't use His divinity to deliver Himself in any way.

When Christ stated, "I thirst," we also see Him identifying and sympathizing with His suffering people. Why do pain, sickness, death, natural disasters, and terrorist destructions exist if God is loving and caring and is the sovereign of this world? The cross reveals that God is not ignorant of our suffering and sorrows. Isaiah stated that He "hath borne our griefs, and carried our sorrows" (Isaiah 53:4).

Suffering is the result of sin. It is sin that has

brought untold suffering and sorrow to this world. It is to end this suffering that Christ died. He died to defeat sin and to end the dire consequences sinners suffer. Because the God we pray to became one of us, we can know that He understands us and sympathizes with us because He has experienced what we experience. "It became him, for whom are all things, and by whom are all things, in bringing many sons unto glory, to make the captain of their salvation perfect through sufferings. . . . Wherefore in all things it [behooved] him to be made like unto his brethren, that he might be a merciful and faithful high priest in things pertaining to God, to make reconciliation for the sins of the people. For in that he himself hath suffered being tempted, he is able to succour them that are tempted" (Hebrews 2:10, 17, 18). "We have not an high priest which cannot be touched with the feeling of our infirmities; but was in all points tempted like as we are, yet without sin. Let us therefore come boldly unto the throne of grace, that we may obtain mercy, and find grace to help in time of need" (Hebrews 4:15, 16).

Discussion Questions

1. **What did Christ's statement "I thirst" indicate about His understanding of Scripture?** _____

_____

2. **What was Christ's desire concerning His life and God's Word?** _____

_____

3. **What did Christ's statement "I thirst" indicate about His purpose to be our Substitute in all things?**

_____

4. **What does Christ's "I thirst" statement reveal about His understanding of the painful experiences we go through?** _____

5. **What should be our attitude concerning God's Word in our lives?** _____

_____

Prayer Focus

Pray for:

- God to fill you with the Holy Spirit.
- God to give you the desire to obey Him in all things.
- Those on your prayer list.

Day 27

The Sixth Saying of Christ on the Cross—Part 1

In today's devotional we will study the sixth saying of Christ on the cross: "When Jesus therefore had received the vinegar, he said, It is finished: and he bowed his head, and gave up the ghost" (John 19:30). The events on the cross were both a tragedy and a triumph. Christ's sixth saying, "It is finished," is not the despairing cry of a dying victim. No, it is a declaration that Christ has victoriously fulfilled the mission He came to do.

Christ had fulfilled the Old Testament prophecies concerning Himself, the Messiah. This fact should give great encouragement to us today. Just as the Old Testament prophecies about Christ's first advent were fulfilled, so also will the prophecies concerning His second coming be fulfilled.

Some may question why it has taken Christ so long to fulfill His promise to return in glory; nearly two thousand years have passed since He promised to return. Remember, from the promise in the Garden of Eden that a Savior would come (Genesis 3:15) to the actual coming of Christ was some four thousand years. We must keep in mind that God has an exact timetable for all events. The first advent of Christ was planned in eternity (see Revelation 13:8), and "when the fullness of the time was come, God sent forth his Son" (Galatians 4:4). Jesus came to planet earth exactly when planned. So His second coming will take place exactly when it was planned to back in eternity. The Father has always known the exact day and hour (see Matthew 24:36).

"It is finished" also declared an end to Christ's suffering. Christ had suffered many things throughout His ministry. He even warned His disciples of the suffering He would endure: "From that time forth began Jesus to [show] unto his disciples, how that he must go unto Jerusalem, and suffer many things of the elders and chief priests and scribes, and be killed, and be raised again the third day" (Matthew 16:21). He must "suffer many things, and be rejected of this generation" (Luke 17:25). He had experienced the struggle in Gethsemane, the mock trial, the scourging, the jeers of priests and people, His disciples forsaking Him, His crucifixion, the severing of His eternal relationship with His Father, and the wrath of God. The more we understand the suffering that Christ endured for us, the stronger will be the love and gratitude we'll feel for Him.

Jesus said that His Father had given Him works that He was to do—works that Jesus said "bear witness of me, that the Father hath sent me" (John 5:36). Now He told the Father, "I have glorified thee on the earth: I have finished the work which thou gavest me to do" (John 17:4). As the disciples declared in their prayer, God had foreordained all the suffering Christ experienced (see Acts 4:27, 28).

God is sovereign; no one can overthrow what He wants done. Satan did everything in his power to keep Christ from fulfilling His mission; but, praise God! Satan failed. In fact, the very suffering that Satan inspired the priests and people to cause Him actually served to fulfill God's purpose in Christ's life. "He doeth according to his will in the army of heaven, and among the inhabitants of the earth: and none can stay his hand, or say unto him, What doest thou?" (Daniel 4:35). "It is finished" echoes through the ages; God's plan will come to a glorious fulfillment.

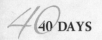

Christ is an example for each of His followers. Are we fulfilling God's purpose in our life as Christ fulfilled His purpose in His life? Do we trust God is all situations and circumstances, whether we perceive them as good or as bad? Do we really believe that God is a sovereign God and that He will fulfill His promise to us that "all things work together for good to them that love God, to them who are the called according to his purpose" (Romans 8:28)?

Discussion Questions

1. **What was finished when Christ said, "It is finished"?** _____ _____

2. **What encouragement should these words concerning Christ's first advent give us concerning His second advent?** _____

3. **What attitude should our understanding of Christ's suffering cause us to have toward Him?** _____

4. **Was it God's will for Christ to suffer as He did?** _____ _____

5. **How should our understanding of God's sovereignty in Christ's life increase our faith when we go through difficult times?** _____

6. **Do you desire to fulfill the purpose God has for you as Christ fulfilled God's purpose in His life?** _____

7. **What do you understand God's purpose in your life to be? Be specific.** _____ _____

Prayer Focus

Pray for:

- **God to fill you with the Holy Spirit.**
- **God to give you the desire to be faithful to Him and to trust Him in all circumstances.**
- **Those on your prayer list.**

The Sixth Saying of Christ on the Cross— Part 2

There's a qualification that those who want to spend eternity with God must meet. They must be righteous and must never have sinned, because "the wages of sin is death" (Romans 6:23). Unfortunately, "there is none righteous, no, not one. . . . For all have sinned, and come short of the glory of God" (Romans 3:10, 23). Therefore, all humankind faces eternal separation from God.

But Jesus' mission was to "seek and . . . save the lost" (Luke 19:10, NIV). When He declared, "It is finished," He proclaimed the accomplishment of our redemption. He had fulfilled the requirement of perfect obedience to God's law; He lived a perfectly sinless life. Peter declared that Jesus "did no sin, neither was guile found in his mouth" (1 Peter 2:22). He overcame every temptation: "We have not an high priest which cannot be touched with the feeling of our infirmities; but was in all points tempted like as we are, yet without sin" (Hebrews 4:15).

Since Jesus obeyed God's law perfectly, He lived a purely righteous life. When Christians put their faith in Him as their Savior, He gives them His perfect righteousness as a "covering," "justifying" righteousness, which is why Paul wrote that his desire was to "be found in him, not having mine own righteousness, which is of the law, but that which is through the faith of Christ, the righteousness which is of God by faith" (Philippians 3:9). Jesus had "finished" the work of righteousness.

As a result, when Jesus declared "It is finished," He was declaring that He had suffered the curse of the law due to sin—which is God's wrath—for us. His cry, "My God, My God, why hast thou forsaken me?" tells us that He had suffered the turning of His Father's face from Him. In other words, our sins had been placed on Him, and He was giving up His life to suffer the death that we deserve so that He could give us the eternal life that was His.

The Greek word translated "finished" is *teleō*, which can have several shades of meaning. In Matthew 11:1, it is translated "made an end." Christ made an end of our sin and guilt, and He provided forgiveness and justification for us. In Matthew 17:24, it is rendered "pay." Jesus paid the price of our sin with His death. In Luke 2:39, *teleō* is translated "performed." Jesus "performed" all the requirements of the law, and thus provided perfect righteousness for us. Luke 18:31 uses the word "accomplish" as a translation of *teleō*. Jesus had accomplished everything the Father had sent Him to achieve. Yes, Jesus had successfully "finished" His mission and made salvation available to His people.

The Father accepted the work of atonement Christ had provided for us. Christ's resurrection confirms the truth that He is the Christ; the Savior of humanity, "and declared to be the Son of God with power, according to the spirit of holiness, by the resurrection from the dead" (Romans 1:4).

The work Christ had finished provided everything we need to be saved. Paul said, "Ye are complete in him, which is the head of all principality and power" (Colossians 2:10). There is nothing we can add to what Christ has done. He is our righteousness. He is our sanctification. And He is our redemption. That's why Paul wrote that "no flesh should glory in his presence. But of him are ye in Christ Jesus, who of God is made unto us wisdom, and righteousness, and sanctification, and redemption: that, according as it is written, He that glorieth, let him glory in the Lord" (1 Corinthians 1:29–31).

"It is finished" is also a declaration that Satan's

power is broken, and his end is sure. Christ has delivered us from the stronghold of Satan's power. He has "delivered us from the power of darkness, and hath translated us into the kingdom of his dear Son" (Colossians 1:13). Because of Christ's victory over sin and the cross, Satan will ultimately be destroyed. Since we are flesh and blood, Jesus "also himself likewise took part of the same; that through death he might destroy him that had the power of death, that is, the devil" (Hebrews 2:14).

Discussion Questions

1. What qualification must those meet who want to spend eternity with God? _____
   _____

2. What did Christ do to meet that requirement for those who believe in Him? _____
   _____

3. How do we know that God the Father accepted the work Christ did for us? _____
   _____

4. Is there anything we can do to add to what Christ has provided for us? _____
   _____

5. What did Christ's victory on the cross do in relation to Satan's power on earth and his destiny?
   _____

Prayer Focus

Pray for:

- God to fill you with the Holy Spirit.
- God to give you the faith to experience the full deliverance from sin that Christ has provided for you.
- Those on your prayer list.

Day 29

The Seventh Saying of Christ on the Cross—Part 1

We have now studied six of Jesus' sayings on the cross. They are, regarding those who were crucifying Him, "Father forgive them for they know not what they do"; to the repentant thief, "Verily I say unto you today, you will be with me in paradise"; to His mother, Mary, "Behold thy son," and to His disciple John, "Behold thy mother"; to His heavenly Father, "My God, My God why hast thou forsaken me?"; to His crucifiers, "I thirst"; and to all who have an interest in the salvation He was providing, "It is finished." Today we will begin considering Christ's seventh and last saying on the cross.

Luke describes the setting and the words: "It was about the sixth hour, and there was a darkness over all the earth until the ninth hour. And the sun was darkened, and the veil of the temple was rent in the midst. And when Jesus had cried with a loud voice, he said, Father, into thy hands I commend my spirit: and having said thus, he gave up the ghost" (Luke 23:44–46).

Three of the preceding six sayings concern human beings, and three are directed to God. The seventh saying indicates completeness, and Christ, having won the battle, now going to rest in the Father's hands. On the seventh day of Creation week, God rested from the work He had done in creating this perfect world for humankind. Similarly, when Christ had done all that needed to be done for our salvation, He rested too—in His Father's hands.

As we have seen, each of the previous six sayings of Christ on the cross was a fulfillment of prophecy. The seventh saying was as well. The psalmist prophetically pictured Christ, in absolute trust, placing Himself in His Father's hands: "In thee, O LORD, do I put my trust; let me never be ashamed: deliver me in thy righteousness. Bow down thine ear to me; deliver me speedily: be thou my strong rock, for an house of defence to save me. For thou art my rock and my fortress; therefore for thy name's sake lead me, and guide me. Pull me out of the net that they have laid privily for me: for thou art my strength. Into thine hand I commit my spirit: thou hast redeemed me, O LORD God of truth" (Psalm 31:1–5).

In this seventh saying we see Christ is back in full communion with the Father. For a time while He was suffering the wrath of God for our sins, the intimate relationship He'd had with the Father had been broken. That's when He had cried out, "My God, My God, why hast thou forsaken me?" Now that awful, painful separation had ended, and following His resurrection He would forever be in full communion with His Father.

This seventh saying once again reveals Christ yielding fully to His Father's will. All throughout His life He had trusted His Father's will and yielded Himself to it. After Jesus' forty days in the wilderness, Satan did all he could to get Jesus to depend upon Himself rather than upon His heavenly Father to meet those temptations. But Jesus didn't turn to His own divinity or presumptuously put Himself in harm's way to prove that He was the Christ. Nor did He bow to Satan to gain the kingdoms of this world (see Matthew 4:1–11). Instead, He yielded to His Father's will and trusted that He would provide for Him.

We should have the same kind of faith in our heavenly Father. Remember the promise He gave to us through Paul: "My God shall supply all your need according to his riches in glory by Christ Jesus" (Philippians 4:19). Therefore, we should "be careful for nothing

[that is, do not worry about anything]; but in every thing by prayer and supplication with thanksgiving let your requests be made known unto God. And the peace of God, which passeth all understanding, shall keep your hearts and minds through Christ Jesus" (verses 6, 7).

During Christ's ministry many things appeared to go wrong. The priests and other leaders of the Jews were constantly criticizing Him and plotting against Him. His disciples seemed slow to understand Him. And even John the Baptist questioned whether Jesus was the Messiah, because He wasn't carrying out the work John believed the Messiah would do. Then, at the end of His ministry Judas betrayed Him, and the Jewish leaders, the Jewish people, and even His disciples forsook Him. There were many times in which Christ could have become very discouraged. But Ellen White pictures Him telling His disciples that whatever circumstances they faced, they should have peace because He has overcome the world (see John 16:33). Then she says, "Christ did not fail, *neither was He discouraged;* and the disciples were to show a faith of the same enduring nature. They were to work as He had worked, depending on Him for strength. Though their way would be obstructed by apparent impossibilities, yet by His grace they were to go forward, despairing of nothing and hoping for everything" (*The Acts of the Apostles,* p. 23; emphasis added).

Christ has set an example for us. Like Him, we should never become discouraged no matter what situation or circumstances we face. Remember, "All things work together for good to them that love God, to them who are the called according to his purpose" (Romans 8:28). God's promises never fail!

Discussion Questions

1. **What was the focus of the first three things Christ said while He was on the cross** _____
   _____

2. **What was the focus of the next three things He said while on the cross?** _____
   _____

3. **What does His seventh saying tell us about Christ's relationship with His Father while He was on the cross?** _____

4. **What lesson does Christ's trusting His Father teach us?** _____
   _____

5. **Why should Christ's followers never become discouraged?** _____
   _____

Prayer Focus
Pray for:

- **God to fill you with the Holy Spirit.**
- **God to give you the faith not to become discouraged in any situation.**
- **Those on your prayer list.**

Day 30

The Seventh Saying of Christ on the Cross—Part 2

In today's devotional we consider again Christ's seventh and final saying on the cross: "It was about the sixth hour, and there was a darkness over all the earth until the ninth hour. And the sun was darkened, and the veil of the temple was rent in the midst. And when Jesus had cried with a loud voice, he said, Father, into thy hands I commend my spirit: and having said thus, he gave up the ghost" (Luke 23:44–46).

Here we see Christ once again yielding His life to His Father, which was the pattern of His entire life. When He was in the temple at twelve years of age, He said, "I must be about my Father's business" (Luke 2:49). In the wilderness when He was tempted to turn the stones to bread to provide for His physical need, instead of deciding to use His divine power to work a miracle on His own behalf, He chose to trust His heavenly Father to provide for His needs. So He met Satan's temptation with the words, "Man shall not live by bread alone, but by every word that proceeds from the mouth of God" (Matthew 4:4). Christ lived a life of absolute dependency upon God.

Christ's seventh saying on the cross is a clear example for us today. Do we yield our will to God and depend on our heavenly Father as Christ did? Do we daily look to God as our provider? Do we yield to God's will even when it appears that to do so will not be in our best interest? Paul instructs us, "Whether therefore ye eat, or drink, or whatsoever ye do, do all to the glory of God" (1 Corinthians 10:31). Our primary goal in life should be to glorify God by being faithful to Him in every walk of life; in the home, at work, in the marketplace, wherever we are. We must learn to trust God as Jesus did.

Jesus gave a very serious warning concerning our focus on material needs. He said, "No man can serve two masters: for either he will hate the one, and love the other; or else he will hold to the one, and despise the other. Ye cannot serve God and mammon" (Matthew 6:24). In this life we cannot serve two gods. We will serve either the god of materialism (mammon) or the true God. Then Jesus connects this warning with the following words:

Therefore I say unto you, Take no thought for your life, what ye shall eat, or what ye shall drink; nor yet for your body, what ye shall put on. Is not the life more than meat, and the body than raiment? Behold the fowls of the air: for they sow not, neither do they reap, nor gather into barns; yet your heavenly Father feedeth them. Are ye not much better than they? Which of you by taking thought can add one cubit unto his stature? And why take ye thought for raiment? Consider the lilies of the field, how they grow; they toil not, neither do they spin: And yet I say unto you, That even Solomon in all his glory was not arrayed like one of these. Wherefore, if God so clothe the grass of the field, which today is, and tomorrow is cast into the oven, shall he not much more clothe you, O ye of little faith? Therefore take no thought, saying, What shall we eat? or, What shall we drink? or, Wherewithal shall we be clothed? (For after all these things do the Gentiles seek:) for your heavenly Father knoweth that ye have need of all these things. But seek ye first the kingdom of God, and his righteousness; and all these things shall be added unto you (Matthew 6:25–33).

Note the word *therefore*. Jesus is saying that if we worry about the necessities of life, we are actually serving the god of materialism (mammon). No, God wants us to focus on Him as a faithful Father who will provide for His children.

Christ's seventh saying on the cross also teaches us that we should not fear death. As David put it, "Though I walk through the valley of the shadow of death, I will fear no evil" (Psalm 23:4). Because of His close communion with His Father, Christ could place Himself in the Father's care as He faced death and the tomb. We see this kind of faith in the three Hebrews as they faced death in Nebuchadnezzar's furnace, and in Daniel when he was threatened with the lion's den, and in Paul and Silas in prison, and in Peter when he was facing execution. God wants us to have peace based on our trust in Him, peace that comes because we rest in His providential care in all circumstances. He wants us to be able to face death without fear because we know the cross of Christ has made our future sure: "For God so loved the world, that he gave his only begotten Son, that whosoever believeth in him should not perish, but have everlasting life" (John 3:16).

Discussion Questions

1. **In what way is the seventh saying of Christ on the cross an example of the pattern He set by His entire life?** _____

   _____

2. **How is Christ's seventh saying on the cross an example for us today?** _____

   _____

3. **What or who are we serving if we worry about the necessities of life?** _____

   _____

4. **Why should Christians be able to face life-threatening situations without fear** _____

   _____

Prayer Focus

Pray for:

- **God to fill you with His Spirit.**
- **God to give you trusting peace in every situation in your life.**
- **Those on your prayer list.**

Lessons
of the Cross

The Garden and the Cross—Part 1

Jesus had just celebrated the Passover and the Communion service. He knew what was about to happen to Himself and His disciples. "When they had sung an hymn, they went out into the mount of Olives. Then saith Jesus unto them, All ye shall be offended because of me this night: for it is written, I will smite the shepherd, and the sheep of the flock shall be scattered abroad. But after I am risen again, I will go before you into Galilee" (Matthew 26:30–32). God knows what lies ahead for each of us as well. In fact, He is preparing a way right now for your deliverance from a crisis that you don't even know about yet.

Peter's response to Christ's warning that the disciples "shall be offended because of me this night" reveals an important truth about Peter and about most other Christians as well. Peter responded, "Though all men shall be offended because of thee, yet will I never be offended" (verse 33). Peter didn't know himself or his own weakness. It is in times of trial that our weaknesses are revealed. Jesus knew the great fall that Peter would experience, and He was warning as well as giving him hope. "The Lord said, Simon, Simon, behold, Satan hath desired to have you, that he may sift you as wheat: But I have prayed for thee, that thy faith fail not: and when thou art converted, strengthen thy brethren" (Luke 22:31, 32).

Just as Jesus interceded for Peter, so also is He interceding for you. He did so in the prayer of His that is recorded in John 17. He said, "Neither pray I for these alone, but for them also which shall believe on me through their word" (verse 20). He also said, "I pray not that thou [the Father] shouldest take them out of the world, but that thou shouldest keep them from the evil" (verse 15). And Jesus continues to intercede for us: "Who is he that condemneth? It is Christ that died, yea rather, that is risen again, who is even at the right hand of God, who also maketh intercession for us" (Romans 8:34).

Following the Passover, Jesus and His disciples made their way to the Garden of Gethsemane. Scripture says,

Then cometh Jesus with them unto a place called Gethsemane, and saith unto the disciples, Sit ye here, while I go and pray yonder. And he took with him Peter and the two sons of Zebedee, and began to be sorrowful and very heavy. Then saith he unto them, My soul is exceeding sorrowful, even unto death: tarry ye here, and watch with me. And he went a little farther, and fell on his face, and prayed, saying, O my Father, if it be possible, let this cup pass from me: nevertheless not as I will, but as thou wilt. And he cometh unto the disciples, and findeth them asleep, and saith unto Peter, What, could ye not watch with me one hour? Watch and pray, that ye enter not into temptation: the spirit indeed is willing, but the flesh is weak. He went away again the second time, and prayed, saying, O my Father, if this cup may not pass away from me, except I drink it, thy will be done. And he came and found them asleep again: for their eyes were heavy. And he left them, and went away again, and prayed the third time, saying the same words (Matthew 26:36–44).

If the disciples had been watching and praying, they would have been prepared for the great crisis that lay

ahead. They would have been prepared for the events associated with the crucifixion of Christ. Prayer always plays a major role in preparing people for any crisis. We see this throughout the ministry of Christ. He often spent entire nights in prayer. As He approached His crucifixion, He felt an even greater desire to pray. He knew that prayer was the only way He could be prepared for the greatest crisis in His life.

Concerning the importance of prayer, Ellen White wrote, "We may leave off many bad habits, for the time we may part company with Satan; but without a vital connection with God, through the surrender of ourselves to Him moment by moment, we shall be overcome. Without a personal acquaintance with Christ, and a continual communion, we are at the mercy of the enemy, and shall do his bidding in the end" (*The Desire of Ages,* p. 324). This is what Paul was recommending when he wrote, "Pray without ceasing" (1 Thessalonians 5:17).

Discussion Questions

1. **What warning did Jesus give to Peter, and what did Jesus say he did in response to this information?**
_____

2. **How did Peter respond to Christ's warning that all the disciples would be offended because of Him? What does this reveal about Peter?** _____
_____

3. **In relation to prayer, what is Jesus doing for you right now?** _____
_____

4. **What should the disciples have done that would have prepared them for the crisis of the cross?**
_____

5. **What did Jesus do throughout His entire ministry and particularly in the Garden of Gethsemane that prepared Him for the cross?** _____
_____

6. **What did Ellen White say we must do in order to remain faithful to God?** _____
_____

Prayer Focus

Pray for:

- **God to fill you with the Holy Spirit.**
- **God to give you the desire to keep a moment-by-moment relationship with Jesus through prayer.**
- **Those on your prayer list.**

Day 32

The Garden and the Cross—Part 2

In yesterday's devotional study we saw that prayer would have prepared the disciples for the events associated with the crucifixion of Christ. Prayer will always play a major role in preparing God's children for the challenges and discouragements of life. Without prayer, our relationship with Christ weakens and our faith falters, and as a result, when the crisis comes, we suffer defeat.

Jesus knew this. That's why He asked His disciples to pray with Him in the Garden of Gethsemane. "Then cometh Jesus with them unto a place called Gethsemane, and saith unto the disciples, Sit ye here, while I go and pray yonder. And he took with him Peter and the two sons of Zebedee, and began to be sorrowful and very heavy. Then saith he unto them, My soul is exceeding sorrowful, even unto death: tarry ye here, and watch with me" (Matthew 26:36–38). When Jesus asked the disciples to sit there while He prayed, and when He took Peter, James, and John a little farther into the Garden and asked them to "watch with Him," He was asking the disciples to pray for and with Him.

It was in the Garden of Gethsemane that Jesus fought the greatest battle He ever faced. The crisis seemed overwhelming. The weight of the sins of the world seemed more than He could bear. The weight of those sins—of our sins—seemed to be crushing the very life out of Him. He told His disciples, "My soul is exceeding sorrowful, even unto death" (verse 38). Christ knew that the only hope He had of making it victoriously through this crisis and the Crucifixion depended on His having the help of His Father.

Christ's humanity shrank back from the enormity of the terrible events that He would soon face. In His humanity He didn't want to go through this crisis. When He felt overwhelmed by it, He prayed to His Father "if it be possible, let this cup pass from me" (verse 39). He knew this was the plan that God had devised for saving His people from their sins. Christ was to be the "Lamb slain from the foundation of the world" (Revelation 13:8). There was no way to bring salvation to humankind except through His bearing their sins and paying the death penalty for them.

However, when it was time for Him to bear this terrible burden, He thought it too heavy. Jesus had always submitted His will to the will of the Father. He had always said, "I seek not mine own will, but the will of the Father which hath sent me" (John 5:30). But the crisis that He was facing now seemed too much for Him to bear. In the face of this crisis, doing His Father's will seemed too much to ask. So He prayed to the Father not just once, but three times, asking Him to, "if it was possible, let this cup pass from me" (Matthew 26:39).

Christ's struggle was over the subordination of His will to the Father's will. So it is with every Christian. It isn't always easy to yield our desires to the will of our heavenly Father. Our sinful nature wants to pull us back into sin. Yet the Holy Spirit moves on our hearts, persuading us to yield to God's will. The struggle may be so great that we, too, may ask our Father to "let this cup pass from me." When we choose to submit our will to God, we will then willingly allow God to crucify self within us. In that moment of surrender, we are "taking up our cross" as Christ admonished us to do. We then experience the resurrection power of Christ and have victory, for "if we have been planted

together in the likeness of his death, we shall be also in the likeness of his resurrection: Knowing this, that our old man is crucified with him, that the body of sin might be destroyed, that henceforth we should not serve sin" (Romans 6:5, 6).

Submission of our will and crucifixion of our sinful self must happen first, for there is no resurrection power without death of self, and there is no wearing of the crown of glory without first bearing the cross. So it was with Christ. Once He submitted His will to the will of the Father, the victory was gained. Then He had the strength to bear the cross, and victory was assured.

If Christ hadn't been victorious in the Garden, there would have been no cross. If there were no cross, there wouldn't have been a glorious resurrection. If there had been no cross and glorious resurrection, then no salvation would have been available for God's children. All would have been lost.

Discussion Questions

1. **If we neglect personal times of prayer with God, what will happen to us spiritually** _____
   _____

2. **What caused Christ to feel so overwhelmed in the Garden of Gethsemane?** _____
   _____

3. **What did Christ ask His Father for in His prayer?** _____
   _____

4. **If Christ hadn't submitted His will to the Father in the Garden, what act essential to our salvation would not have taken place?** _____
   _____

5. **Why are our personal times with God in prayer essential to our gaining the victory over future temptations?** _____

6. **How do we submit our wills to God?** _____
   _____

Prayer Focus

Pray for:

- **God to fill you with the Holy Spirit.**
- **God to give you the desire to yield your will to Him when you struggle with temptation.**
- **Those on your prayer list.**

Day 33

The Shame of the Cross

Death on a cross was a shameful death. The Bible clearly declares "he that is hanged is accursed of God" (Deuteronomy 21:23). People of that time considered anyone who died on a cross to have been cursed and forsaken by God. Thus, they were also considered to be vile sinners without any hope of salvation. They were a shame to their families and brought great disgrace upon them. It was in part because of these views of crucifixion that the Jewish leaders believed Christ couldn't be the Messiah since He died on a cross.

Following Jesus' resurrection, He joined two individuals on the road to Emmaus. They didn't recognize who He was as He walked with them. When He asked why they were sad, they said Jesus of Nazareth was a prophet mighty in deed and word before God and all the people. And then they said the chief priests and their rulers delivered Jesus to be condemned to death and crucified, when they had trusted that He was the One who would redeem Israel (see Luke 24:19–21). They didn't understand how Jesus could be the Messiah since He was crucified, which they believed meant that God had cursed Him.

The Christian belief that Jesus died on a cross is also one of the reasons Muslims reject Christianity. They believe that Allah wouldn't allow one of his prophets to die in such a disgraceful manner. Instead, Muslims teach that Jesus was rescued—saved from going to the cross (see Koran 4:157).

In the view of the people who were contemporaries of Jesus, dying on a cross was nothing to celebrate. Rather, it was a disgrace to be forgotten. So, Jesus' dying on a cross was an incomprehensible barrier to considering Him to be the Messiah. Such a death clearly indicated that He must not have been who He claimed to be.

It is so often the case that people—even those who believe in God—misunderstand what He says and what He does. Such was true of Jesus' crucifixion. Paul declared this truth with these words: "O the depth of the riches both of the wisdom and knowledge of God! how unsearchable are his judgments, and his ways past finding out!" (Romans 11:33).

However, once the event has taken place and believers can reflect on its significance, the Holy Spirit enlightens them. Such was the case of the cross. Paul clearly proclaimed the significance of the cross of Christ when he wrote, "Christ hath redeemed us from the curse of the law, being made a curse for us: for it is written, Cursed is every one that hangeth on a tree" (Galatians 3:13). Christ died on the cross to redeem us from the "curse" of God, which we deserve because of our sin.

When Christ died on the cross, the Lord "laid on him the iniquity of us all" (Isaiah 53:6). Christ was bearing our sins when He hung on the cross. He suffered the curse of God for us. He experienced the separation from God that sin causes—the separation that forced from Him the cry, "My God, my God, why hast thou forsaken me?" (Matthew 27:46). Jesus experienced the separation from God that sinners suffer.

The Bible tells us that the "wages of sin is death" (Romans 6:23). Sinners deserve the separation from God that results in eternal death. Jesus didn't bear the curse of God and die the death of a sinner on the cross because of sins He had committed, for He hadn't sinned (see 1 Peter 2:22). The curse of God, the death

Christ died, was for our sins. It is because of this that God could declare, "Ye shall know that I am in the midst of Israel, and that I am the LORD your God, and none else: and my people shall never be ashamed" (Joel 2:27). Through the prophet Joel, God foretold that when the I AM appeared in Israel, He would take upon Himself the "shame" of His people so they would never have to bear that shame themselves.

Because of the great victory over sin that Christ obtained for all who believe in Him, what had been a symbol of great shame became the symbol of a marvelous sacrifice, of a great love. The cross of Christ became something to glory in, to rejoice in, and to proclaim to the world. Paul stated it well: "God forbid that I should glory, save in the cross of our Lord Jesus Christ" (Galatians 6:14).

Discussion Questions

1. **What kind of death was that of dying on a cross** _____
_____

2. **Why was it so difficult for the Jewish leaders to believe that the Messiah would die on a cross?**
_____

3. **Can God's people always understand what He does? Explain your answer.** _____
_____

4. **What did Christ's death on a cross say to the people of His time? What does it say to us?** ____
_____

5. **When Christ died on the cross, what was He doing for us?** _____
_____

6. **Why do Christians glory in the cross?** _____
_____

Prayer Focus

Pray for:

- **God to fill you with His Spirit.**
- **God to deepen your understanding of Christ's sacrifice for you on the cross.**
- **Those on your prayer list.**

Day 34

Lazarus and the Cross

Many members of the Jewish leadership—scribes, Pharisees, priests, etc.—were very concerned about what Jesus was teaching, and they were constantly trying to prove that Jesus was an imposter who was leading the people astray. Since these Jewish leaders considered themselves to be protectors of the people, they kept trying to find a way to stop Jesus' ministry.

In the Gospel of John we read of an amazing miracle: the restoring to life of Lazarus, the brother of Martha and Mary (see John 11:20–44). Many people knew this family and were there when Lazarus was resurrected. We are told that as a result of this miracle, many of the Jews "believed on him [Jesus]" (verse 45). However, others were there because they were spies for the Pharisees. They "went their ways to the Pharisees, and told them what things Jesus had done" (verse 46). We will see that this miracle and the cross of Christ are closely related.

This miracle greatly concerned the leaders of the Jews, so they called a meeting to decide what to do about Jesus. John wrote, "Then gathered the chief priests and the Pharisees a council, and said, What do we? for this man doeth many miracles. If we let him thus alone, all men will believe on him: and the Romans shall come and take away both our place and nation" (verses 47, 48). These leaders had learned that just as God punished His people by sending them into the Babylonian captivity when they accepted idolatry and false teachings, so God would punish them in much the same way if they drifted away from Him again. The leaders feared that if the people continued to follow Jesus, the same thing would happen. So the high priest, "one of them, named Caiaphas, . . . said unto them, Ye know nothing at all,

nor consider that it is expedient for us, that one man should die for the people, and that the whole nation perish not. And this spake he not of himself: but being high priest that year, he prophesied that Jesus should die for that nation; and not for that nation only, but that also he should gather together in one the children of God that were scattered abroad" (verses 49–52). They then made their decision: "from that day forth they took counsel together for to put him to death" (verse 53). And as if that wasn't enough, they added another task—"the chief priests consulted that they might put Lazarus also to death; because that by reason of him many of the Jews went away, and believed on Jesus" (John 12:10, 11).

In the raising of Lazarus from the dead we see several important truths. First, the resurrection of Lazarus became the catalyst that led to the cross of Christ. Satan used one of Jesus' greatest miracles—which we might think would convince all that He was the Messiah—to motivate people to crucify Him. In fact, the Jewish leaders had attributed Jesus' miracles to the devil. As Matthew put it: "This fellow doth not cast out devils, but by Beelzebub the prince of the devils" (Matthew 12:24). Jesus declared that their statement was a "blasphemy against the Holy Ghost" (verse 31). Hence, to attribute the work of the Holy Spirit to the devil is blasphemy.

In these last days we need to be very careful that we don't judge miracles too quickly. We know that Satan will use false miracles to lead men and women astray (see, for example, Matthew 24:24; Revelation 16:14). However, we also know that there are true miracles (see, for example, 1 Corinthians 12:9, 10), and the book of Acts tells us that the disciples performed many miracles. In addition, Ellen White saw in vision a great

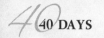

"reformatory movement among God's people" in the last days, accompanied by the healing of the sick and other miracles (*Christian Service,* p. 42).

This story holds another lesson for us—a warning. Though the high priest was directly involved in plotting the death of Jesus, God still honored the position he held. Scripture tells us "this spake he not of himself: but being high priest that year, he prophesied that Jesus should die for that nation; and not for that nation only, but that also he should gather together in one the children of God that were scattered abroad" (John 11:51, 52).

In both the Old and New Testaments, God gives severe warnings against our speaking against or working against God's ordained leadership, even if we don't think they are doing a good job. God sets up kings and takes down kings (see Daniel 2:21). Our part is to pray for those in leadership (1 Timothy 2:1–3).

Another important lesson in Jesus' raising of Lazarus is that He didn't immediately respond to Martha's and Mary's request for Him to come and heal their brother. He waited until Lazarus had died because He wanted to show people that He is more than just a healer of disease. Jesus wanted Martha and Mary to know that He is also "the resurrection and the life" (John 11:25). We must learn to wait on God in prayer, for it may be then that we will receive an even greater blessing than the one for which we are asking. Ellen White wrote, "In the future life the mysteries that here have annoyed and disappointed us will be made plain. We shall see that our seemingly unanswered prayers and disappointed hopes have been among our greatest blessings" (*The Ministry of Healing,* p. 474).

Discussion Questions

1. **What miracle did Jesus perform that especially concerned the Pharisees and priests** _____
   _____

2. **What decision did the Jewish leaders make as a result of this miracle?** _____
   _____

3. **In the context of miracles, what did Jesus say about blasphemy against the Holy Spirit?** ____
   _____

4. **How should we relate to miracles in our day?** _____
   _____

5. **How should we relate to leadership with which we don't agree?** _____
   _____

Prayer Focus
Pray for:

- **God to fill you with His Spirit.**
- **God to give you spiritual discernment to know His will concerning miracles, to remind you to pray for leadership, and to help you learn to wait on God in prayer.**
- **Those on your prayer list.**

Day 35

Legalism and the Cross

Satan has always tried to supplant Christ. He started a war in heaven and continued it on the battlefield of this earth, targeting especially God's people. Legalism is one of Satan's means of supplanting Christ. Legalists rely on their own efforts to be saved rather than relying on Christ. It may be surprising to realize, but legalism actually played a role in placing Christ on the cross.

As we saw in a previous devotional, the Jewish leaders were very concerned about Jesus' teaching that salvation came through belief in Him. You see, the Jewish leaders had learned the hard lessons of the Babylonian captivity. They knew that God had punished Israel because that nation had broken God's law. So when the Jews returned from their captivity in Babylon, the members of the Pharisee sect of Judaism became the protectors of God's law. They determined that they would set up restrictions that they then commanded people to obey, thinking these human laws would prevent God's people from wandering away from God and His law another time. It is these "commandments of men" and not God's Ten Commandment law that Jesus was accused of breaking.

Knowing that these human laws had no authority, Jesus often spoke against them as He tried to lead the people of God back to His law and to point to Himself as the means of salvation. One example of Jesus addressing the false teachings is found in Matthew 15:

Then came to Jesus scribes and Pharisees, which were of Jerusalem, saying, Why do thy disciples transgress the tradition of the elders? for they wash not their hands when they eat bread. But he answered and said unto them, Why do ye also transgress the commandment of God by your tradition? For God commanded, saying, Honour thy father and mother: and, He that curseth father or mother, let him die the death. But ye say, Whosoever shall say to his father or his mother, It is a gift, by whatsoever thou mightest be profited by me; and honour not his father or his mother, he shall be free. Thus have ye made the commandment of God of none effect by your tradition. Ye hypocrites, well did Esaias prophesy of you, saying, This people draweth nigh unto me with their mouth, and honoureth me with their lips; but their heart is far from me. But in vain they do worship me, teaching for doctrines the commandments of men (Matthew 15:1–9).

Also, Jesus pointed to Himself many times as the way of salvation. For example, He told Thomas, "I am the way, the truth, and the life: no man cometh unto the Father, but by me" (John 14:6).

Because Jesus rejected the Jewish leaders' teaching on legalistic obedience and their traditions, they became very concerned that He was leading the people astray, which would once again bring God's wrath upon His people. So we read that in their committee meeting "one of them, named Caiaphas, being the high priest that same year, said unto them, Ye know nothing at all, nor consider that it is expedient for us, that one man should die for the people, and that the whole nation perish not" (John 11:49, 50). Hence, we see that their legalistic teachings led them to plan the death of Jesus.

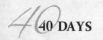

The apostle Paul understood why the Jewish leaders rejected Jesus and had Him crucified. He told us their motivation: "Israel, which followed after the law of righteousness, hath not attained to the law of righteousness. Wherefore? Because they sought it not by faith, but as it were by the works of the law. For they stumbled at that stumblingstone; as it is written, Behold, I lay in Sion a stumblingstone and rock of offence: and whosoever believeth on him shall not be ashamed" (Romans 9:31–33). God even foretold that this would happen: "Sanctify the LORD of hosts himself; and let him be your fear, and let him be your dread. And he shall be for a sanctuary; but for a stone of stumbling and for a rock of offence to both the houses of Israel, for a gin and for a snare to the inhabitants of Jerusalem. And many among them shall stumble, and fall, and be broken, and be snared, and be taken" (Isaiah 8:13–15).

The warning is for us today also. Let us not fall into the falsehood of legalism, looking to ourselves for victory over sin and thus to stumble at the "stumbling stone"—the rock Jesus Christ. If we do, the cross of Christ will be of none effect for us. Paul is clear on the matter: "No flesh should glory in his presence. But of him are ye in Christ Jesus, who of God is made unto us wisdom, and righteousness, and sanctification, and redemption: That, according as it is written, He that glorieth, let him glory in the Lord" (1 Corinthians 1:29–31).

Discussion Questions

1. **Who is Satan always trying to supplant?** _____

2. **What did the Jewish leaders think Jesus was doing that caused them to plan His death** _____

   _____

3. **How did the Jewish leaders believe salvation was to be gained** _____

   _____

4. **What did Jesus teach that caused such concern among the Jewish leaders?** _____

   _____

5. **Are you in danger of looking to legalistic obedience instead of to Jesus for your salvation?** ___

   _____

Prayer Focus

Pray for:

- God to fill you with His Spirit.
- God to open your eyes to the truth that full and complete salvation is found in Jesus Christ.
- Those on your prayer list.

Day 36

The Cross's Warning to Religious Leaders

It is sad but true that many professed religious leaders have not known what God was doing in their day. There were religious leaders in Noah's day, yet, we find none of them in the ark. Only Noah and his family were saved from the Flood. There were religious leaders in Sodom and Gomorrah, yet when God sent destruction upon those two cities, only Lot and his two daughters escaped it. Jesus was speaking of Jewish religious leaders of the past when He declared that "Jerusalem" killed the prophets and stoned those who were sent to them (see Matthew 23:37). The same thing was true in Christ's day as well—the vast majority of the religious leaders of Christ's day rejected Him, the very "I AM" (John 8:58) of the Old Testament.

It was because the religious leaders of Christ's day didn't know what God was doing in their midst that they were responsible for putting Him on the cross. When Jesus was born, they didn't recognize Him as God "manifest in the flesh" (1 Timothy 3:16). When angels came to earth to announce the birth of Jesus, it was to a few shepherds and not to the religious leaders of Judah that they brought the news. The precious gifts Jesus received as the newborn King of the Jews came from wise men from the east, not Jewish aristocrats. And it was the Jewish leaders who plotted the death of Jesus following the resurrection of Lazarus. At that time, "the chief priests and the Pharisees [gathered in] a council, and said, What do we? for this man doeth many miracles. If we let him thus alone, all men will believe on him: and the Romans shall come and take away both our place and nation. And one of them, named Caiaphas, being the high priest that same year, said unto them, Ye know nothing at all, nor consider that it is expedient for us, that one man should die for the people, and that the whole nation perish not" John 11:47–50).

The same sad story is true beyond the New Testament era. The religious leaders of the dominant church during the time of the Protestant Reformation didn't know what God was doing and found themselves fighting against God. When God brought about the Advent awakening in the 1840s and onward, the majority of church leaders spoke and worked against this moving of God among His people. This has been true in my own denomination (the Seventh-day Adventist Church) too. For instance, at the General Conference session held in 1888, God called the church to preach righteousness by faith. But many of the denominational leaders opposed the message, not recognizing that it came from God.

History and the cross give a serious warning to religious leaders as well as to the lay members of the Christian churches of every era. It is absolutely essential we be filled with and led by the Spirit of God, and that we not be too quick to reject the messages and messengers that come to us. We all need to be like the Bereans, of whom we read, "These were more noble than those in Thessalonica, in that they received the word with all readiness of mind, and searched the scriptures daily, whether those things were so" (Acts 17:11). Whenever we hear or read a message that professes to be from God, we must compare it with God's Word. If it agrees with God's Word, we must accept it. If it doesn't, then we are to reject it.

One of the gifts promised to those who are filled with the Holy Spirit is discernment (1 Corinthians

12:10). This gift will protect us from being misled. We can trust God to guide us into all truth by His Spirit (John 16:13).

We need this gift, for Jesus warned that in the last days "there shall arise false Christs, and false prophets, and shall [show] great signs and wonders; insomuch that, if it were possible, they shall deceive the very elect" (Matthew 24:24). And Ellen White has written regarding Satan's last deception: "Only those who have been diligent students of the Scriptures and who have received the love of the truth will be shielded from the powerful delusion that takes the world captive. By the

Bible testimony these will detect the deceiver in his disguise" (*The Great Controversy,* p. 625).

The religious leaders of Christ's day could have recognized Him when He came. They had the Old Testament scriptures, which contained many prophecies about the Messiah's appearance. They had the sanctuary and its services, which all pointed to the Christ. The cross of Christ warns us all that we must have the Spirit's guidance as we study God's Word, and we must allow Him to lead us if we are to avoid being misled as so many of God's professed religious leaders and people were in Christ's day.

Discussion Questions

1. **List some specific occasions when professed religious leaders and people were unaware of what God was doing in their day.** _____

_____

2. **Why didn't the religious leaders of Christ's day understand what God was doing through Jesus Christ** _____

3. **Why were the Bereans more noble than the people in Thessalonica?** _____

_____

4. **What must we do to be sure we are not deceived in these last days** _____

_____

Prayer Focus
Pray for:

- **God to fill you with His Spirit.**
- **God to guide you by His Spirit in your life and as you study His Word.**
- **Those on your prayer list.**

The Cross and the Ten Commandments

If there were no Ten Commandments, there would be no need for the cross of Christ. Why is that true? It is true because the Ten Commandments define sin. Paul wrote, "What shall we say then? Is the law sin? God forbid. Nay, I had not known sin, but by the law: for I had not known lust, except the law had said, Thou shalt not covet" (Romans 7:7). In this text Paul states that it is the law of God that tells us what sin is.

What law was Paul referring to? The answer is clear. In this statement, Paul quotes the tenth commandment, which prohibits coveting (see Exodus 20:17). In Romans 7, Paul goes on to clarify his statement that the law is not sin. He states that to the contrary, "the law is holy, and the commandment holy, and just, and good" (verse 12). The Ten Commandments define God's holy, just, and good will for our behavior. People who are holy, just, and good will obey God's law perfectly. In fact, these adjectives—holy, just, and good—are used to define God Himself. "The LORD our God is holy" (Psalm 99:9). "There is no God else beside me; a just God" (Isaiah 45:21). "The LORD is good" (Psalm 100:5).

Sinful behavior is the opposite of holy, just, and good behavior. Therefore, whenever someone speaks or acts contrary to the Ten Commandments, they have behaved sinfully. John declared, "Whosoever committeth sin transgresseth also the law: for sin is the transgression of the law" (1 John 3:4). If there were no Ten Commandment law, which defines sin, there would be no sin. Paul stated this clearly: "Where no law is, there is no transgression" (Romans 4:15).

Therefore, the Bible is very clear that the Ten Commandments define what sin is and that when people disobey one of the Ten Commandments, they sin. In fact, James points out that when we break one of the Ten Commandments, we break all of them: "Whosoever shall keep the whole law, and yet offend in one point, he is guilty of all. For he that said, Do not commit adultery, said also, Do not kill. Now if thou commit no adultery, yet if thou kill, thou art become a transgressor of the law. So speak ye, and so do, as they that shall be judged by the law of liberty" (James 2:10–12).

This text in James presents two very important truths. First, the Ten Commandments comprise the law that every man and woman will be judged by to determine whether or not they are sinners. And second, notice also that here James calls the Ten Commandments the "law of liberty." Satan wants us to think that the Ten Commandments limit our liberty or freedom. The truth is the law of God actually brings liberty to all. Just think what your neighborhood would be like if everyone who lived there and all those who passed through it kept the Ten Commandments. Would you have more or less liberty? You would have more liberty, of course. Why? Because you would never be afraid of someone breaking into your home or someone attacking you. Your neighborhood would be the most desirable one in your city.

What does all this have to do with the cross of Christ? Christ died for our sins—our breaking of the Ten Commandments. The Bible is clear on two important facts concerning human beings and Christ's death. First, all of us have sinned: "All have sinned, and come short of the glory of God" (Romans 3:23). And second, "Christ died for our sins according to the

scriptures" (1 Corinthians 15:3). You see, the just penalty for our sin is death: "The wages of sin is death" (Romans 6:23). Christ's death on the cross was payment for sin; but our sin, not His, for He had no sin. He kept the Ten Commandments perfectly. Christ the sinless One died for us the sinful ones. Therefore, if we have faith in Christ as our Savior, we will not have to suffer the just penalty for our sins. Instead, we will receive His eternal life. "For God so loved the world, that he gave his only begotten Son, that whosoever believeth in him should not perish, but have everlasting life" (John 3:16). Note also that our faith that Christ saves us from our lawbreaking affirms the fact that the Ten Commandments are still in effect. Paul wrote that we don't make the law void through faith. "God forbid: yea, we establish the law" (Romans 3:31).

In summary, if there were no Ten Commandments, there would be no sin. If there were no sin, there would be no death penalty for the sinner. If there were no death penalty, there would have been no need for the cross of Christ. Hence, the Ten Commandments and the cross of Christ are inseparable. The cross of Christ declares the Ten Commandments unchangeable and eternal.

Discussion Questions

1. **What adjectives does the Bible use to describe both God and the Ten Commandments?** _____

2. **What do the Ten Commandments define?** _____

3. **When we break the Ten Commandments, what are we doing?** _____

4. **What is the just penalty for breaking the Ten Commandments?** _____

5. **How are the Ten Commandments and the cross of Christ related?** _____

6. **Why would there be no need for the cross of Christ if there were no Ten Commandments?** _____

7. **Why does the Bible call the Ten Commandments the "law of liberty"?** _____

Prayer Focus

Pray for:

- **God to fill you with the Holy Spirit.**
- **God to help you clearly understand the relationship between the Ten Commandments and the cross of Christ.**
- **Those on your prayer list.**

Day 38

The Cross and the Ceremonial Law

There are several sets of laws in the Bible. The two laws related to the cross that I am focusing on are the Ten Commandments, or moral law, and the ceremonial law. We have considered the Ten Commandments and the cross. In today's devotional we will focus on the ceremonial law.

In the Old Testament, God gave Israel a set of ceremonial laws, which are also called types and shadows (Hebrews 10:1). They were laws that pointed to Christ. For example, God told Moses, "Let them make me a sanctuary; that I may dwell among them" (Exodus 25:8). This sanctuary where God dwelt among His people pointed to a time when Christ would come in person and dwell among His people. John wrote of this in these terms: "The Word was made flesh, and dwelt among us, (and we beheld his glory, the glory as of the only begotten of the Father,) full of grace and truth" (John 1:14). A synonym to the word *dwelt* is *tabernacled*, which refers to the Old Testament tabernacle— the place of God's dwelling among His people.

The Old Testament tabernacle and its services all pointed to Christ. They were "shadows" pointing to a reality, Jesus Christ. This is why Christ told the Jewish leaders, "Destroy this temple, and in three days I will raise it up" (John 2:19). Here Jesus clearly referred to Himself as the "temple." Every article in the Old Testament temple pointed to Christ. The lampstands and the light they gave off pointed to Jesus, who said, "I am the light of the world: he that followeth me shall not walk in darkness, but shall have the light of life" (John 8:12). The table of shewbread symbolized Jesus, for He stated: "I am the bread of life: he that cometh to me shall never hunger; and he that believeth on me shall never thirst" (John 6:35).

Every article of furniture in the temple foreshadowed Jesus. Even the ark of the covenant in the Most Holy Place of the temple pointed to Him. The Ten Commandments were kept inside the ark, and the Shekinah glory—the visible presence of the infinite, holy, all-powerful God Himself—rose above the gold cover of the ark. So the "mercy seat" intervened between the Ten Commandments, broken by sinful humans, and the fiery holiness of God. John referred to this aspect of Jesus' ministry when he wrote, "My little children, these things write I unto you, that ye sin not. And if any man sin, we have an advocate with the Father, Jesus Christ the righteous: And he is the propitiation for our sins: and not for ours only, but also for the sins of the whole world" (1 John 2:1, 2). The Greek word translated "propitiation" in verse 2 is translated "mercy seat" in Hebrews 9:5. Christ was the "mercy seat."

One very important part of the Old Testament ceremonial law was the sacrificial system. If, for example, a man had sinned and wanted God's forgiveness, he would bring a lamb, confess the sin over the head of the lamb, and then kill the lamb. This sacrifice and those that the priests offered for the all the people every morning and evening were meant to remind God's people that the penalty for breaking God's law was death. But even more important, these ceremonial sacrifices all pointed to Christ, whom John the Baptist called "the Lamb of God, which taketh away the sin of the world" (John 1:29).

Jesus Christ was the Lamb of God whose death was symbolically represented by the ceremonial law's

95

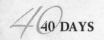

sacrificial system. Every lamb brought as a sacrifice by someone seeking forgiveness for his or her sin pointed to the cross of Christ. Every morning sacrifice and every evening sacrifice offered was pointing to the cross of Christ. Hence, the sanctuary and services of the Old Testament ceremonial law were types and shadows of a reality that was to come: Jesus Christ. The Lamb of God and cross of Christ were central to the reality to which they all pointed. Once the reality (Jesus) came, the types and shadows—the ceremonial laws—were no longer needed. That is why in his Gospel, Matthew tells us that when Jesus died, "the veil of the temple was rent in twain from the top to the bottom" (Matthew 27:51). This veil had separated the Holy Place from the Most Holy Place. Its being torn from top to bottom indicated that the temple and its services were fulfilled in the person of Jesus Christ.

Discussion Questions

1. What did the Old Testament ceremonial law include? _____
   _____

2. Why are the ceremonial laws called "types" and "shadows"? _____
   _____

3. What reality did the lampstand, shewbread, mercy seat, and sacrificial lamb point to? _____
   _____

4. What did John the Baptist call Jesus? _____
   _____

5. What is the relationship between the ceremonial laws and the cross of Christ? _____
   _____

6. What happened to the veil in the temple when Jesus died, and what did this indicate? _____
   _____

Prayer Focus

Pray for:

- God to fill you with the Holy Spirit.
- God to put a deep thankfulness in your heart for the Lamb of God who has paid the price for your sins.
- Those on your prayer list.

Day 39

The Cross and the Sabbath

Genesis 1 describes the first six days of Creation, and each day ends with the words "the evening and the morning" followed by the number of the day just described. This portrayal of the first six days of Creation informs us that our God is the God who creates. And by ending each day's story with the words "the evening and the morning," God is telling us that the work of creating on that day is complete. The work of creation done on that day was not to be repeated.

When we have read all that it says about the sixth day of Creation, the next verses say, "Thus the heavens and the earth were finished, and all the host of them. And on the seventh day God ended his work which he had made; and he rested on the seventh day from all his work which he had made. And God blessed the seventh day, and sanctified it: because that in it he had rested from all his work which God created and made" (Genesis 2:1–3). These verses tell us that our God is not only the One who created, but He is also the One who makes holy, for we are told that He "blessed the seventh day, and sanctified it." God sanctified or made holy the seventh day. He is the God who makes holy.

It is important that we note that the Bible doesn't say "the evening and the morning were the seventh day" at the end of the description of what God did on the seventh day. Why doesn't the description of what God did on the seventh day end the same way as the other six days? It doesn't end the same way because while God finished what He created on each of the first six days, He didn't complete what He created on the seventh day. The story of what He created on the seventh day doesn't end with the expression "the evening and the morning" because God's work of making what

He created on that day holy wasn't complete. His plan was to, in time, make Adam and Eve holy.

At the end of the sixth day of creation we are told that "God saw every thing that he had made, and, behold, it was very good. And the evening and the morning were the sixth day" (Genesis 1:31). God declared that what He created on that day—including Adam and Eve—were "good," but they weren't yet holy. If Adam and Eve had remained faithful to God, they would have grown in their personal relationship with Him and their obedience to Him. They would have grown into a "holy" pair.

However, the sad truth is that Adam and Eve didn't achieve the high and holy relationship God had planned for them. But their fall into sin didn't change God's plan to make humans holy. In both the Old and New Testament, God's people are called to be "holy." "Sanctify yourselves therefore, and be ye holy: for I am the LORD your God" (Leviticus 20:7). "As he which hath called you is holy, so be ye holy in all manner of conversation; because it is written, Be ye holy; for I am holy" (1 Peter 1:15, 16).

This is what the cross of Christ was all about. Christ took the sins of His people upon Himself and suffered the punishment they incurred, which is death. Because of the cross we can become a holy, obedient people unto God as we choose to let Jesus live out His holy, obedient life in us. Concerning this, Peter wrote, "Ye also, as lively stones, are built up a spiritual house, an holy priesthood, to offer up spiritual sacrifices, acceptable to God by Jesus Christ. . . . But ye are a chosen generation, a royal priesthood, an holy nation, a peculiar people; that ye should show forth the praises

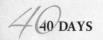

of him who hath called you out of darkness into his marvelous light: which in time past were not a people, but are now the people of God: which had not obtained mercy, but now have obtained mercy" (1 Peter 2:5, 9, 10). Because of the cross of Christ we are called to be a "holy priesthood" and a "holy nation." The cross of Christ made this possible.

When in the story of Creation God is said to be making the seventh day holy and the description of the day doesn't end with the words the "evening and morning," we see that His work of making holy was not completed on that day. God's work of making His people holy was to extend beyond that seventh day. This is why in the message God gave to the prophet Ezekiel to pass along to His people He said, "I gave them my sabbaths, to be a sign between me and them, that they might know that I am the LORD that sanctify them" (Ezekiel 20:12). Every time we follow God's command to "keep holy the Sabbath day" (see Exodus 20:8), we are celebrating God's work of making His people holy. And every time we follow this command, we are celebrating the cross of Christ, which was essential to God's people becoming a holy people.

Discussion Questions

1. **What was God indicating when He had the biblical description of each of the first six days of Creation end with the expression "the evening and the morning"?** _____

_____

2. **What does the creation of the seventh day tell us about God?** _____

_____

3. **The ending of the accounts of all of the first six days of Creation includes the words "the evening and the morning." What was God indicating when He didn't use this expression at the end of the description of His sanctifying the seventh day (making it holy)?** _____

_____

4. **What kind of people does God want us to be?** _____

5. **What role does the cross of Christ play in God's people becoming holy?** _____

_____

6. **What relationship is there between the seventh-day Sabbath, holiness, and the cross?**

_____

Prayer Focus

Pray for:

- **God to fill you with the Holy Spirit.**
- **God to lead you to become a holy, obedient follower of Jesus Christ.**
- **Those on your prayer list.**

Day 40

Glory in the Cross

The cross of Christ has depths of meaning and significance that will be our study throughout the endless ages of eternity. The more we know about the cross of Christ, the more we will be filled with praise to God. Paul expressed the impact the cross had on his life when he wrote, "God forbid that I should glory, save in the cross of our Lord Jesus Christ, by whom the world is crucified unto me, and I unto the world" (Galatians 6:14). The Greek word translated "glory" means to boast in and to exalt above other things.

In this devotional we have seen that the cross of Christ is the greatest revelation of God's love. Because of Christ's sacrifice on the cross, Satan's true character has been revealed. As a result of this revelation of God's love and Satan's evil character, sin and Satan have been defeated and will someday be dead and gone forever.

The cross of Christ makes possible the complete reconciliation between God and man that was lost through Adam's sin in the Garden of Eden: "It pleased the Father that in him [Christ] should all fullness dwell; and, having made peace through the blood of his cross, by him to reconcile all things unto himself; by him, I say, whether they be things in earth, or things in heaven" (Colossians 1:20).

For believers, Christ's cross brings freedom from the guilt and the penalty (death) of sin, and gives them eternal life. On the cross Jesus took upon Himself our sins and paid the penalty for them. Because of this we can receive the eternal life He deserves. "For God so loved the world, that he gave his only begotten Son, that whosoever believeth in him should not perish, but have everlasting life" (John 3:16).

When Jesus died and was buried, the old sinful you died and was buried with Him. Therefore, you no longer have to be controlled by your sinful nature. You can be free from its power. "Our old man is crucified with him, that the body of sin might be destroyed, that henceforth we should not serve sin. . . . Likewise reckon ye also yourselves to be dead indeed unto sin, but alive unto God through Jesus Christ our Lord. Let not sin therefore reign in your mortal body, that ye should obey it in the lusts thereof. Neither yield ye your members as instruments of unrighteousness unto sin: but yield yourselves unto God, as those that are alive from the dead, and your members as instruments of righteousness unto God" (Romans 6:6, 11–13).

If Christ hadn't died, there would have been no burial. If there was no burial, there would have been no glorious resurrection and exaltation of Christ to the right hand of the Father, which allowed the Holy Spirit to be poured out in power on the Day of Pentecost. From that day forward the baptism of the Holy Spirit became available to all believers, and it is through Him that Christ dwells most fully in His followers. Jesus made this truth clear. After He told the disciples about the coming of the Comforter, which is the experience of the baptism of the Holy Spirit, Jesus said, "I will not leave you comfortless; I will come to you" (see John 14:16–18).

It is through the baptism of the Holy Spirit that Jesus dwells in us most fully. When He does, He can then become the source of our victory over temptation. Paul was describing this blessing when he wrote, "I am crucified with Christ: nevertheless I live; yet not I, but Christ liveth in me: and the life which I now live in the

flesh I live by the faith of the Son of God, who loved me, and gave himself for me" (Galatians 2:20).

The cross of Christ made it possible for the mystery of God that had been hid until now to become known—"even the mystery which hath been hid from ages and from generations, but now is made manifest to his saints: to whom God would make known what is the riches of the glory of this mystery among the Gentiles; which is Christ in you, the hope of glory" (Colossians 1:26, 27). It is because of the cross that Christ can live in you.

Because of the suffering for our sins that Christ endured, we can be delivered from the spiritual, emotional, and physical consequences of our sin. Jesus declared, "If the Son . . . shall make you free, ye shall be free indeed" (John 8:36). We can be made whole and even experience the abundant life in the present. Jesus said, "I am come that they might have life, and that they might have it more abundantly" (John 10:10).

The list of blessings the cross of Christ provides could go on and on. Throughout eternity we shall see even greater blessings of the cross. Ellen White declared; "The cross of Christ will be the science and the song of the redeemed through all eternity" (*The Great Controversy,* p. 651). May we each with Paul glory in the cross of Christ.

Discussion Questions

1. **What did Paul mean when he said he would glory only in the cross of Christ?** _____

_____

2. **What does the cross reveal about God?** _____

_____

3. **What reconciliation does the cross bring about?** _____

_____

4. **How does the cross free you from the guilt, penalty, and power of sin in your life?** _____

_____

5. **What does the cross of Christ have to do with the baptism of the Holy Spirit?** _____

_____

6. **What deliverance is available to you because of the cross of Christ?** _____

_____

7. **What will be the science and song of the redeemed throughout eternity?** _____

_____

Prayer Focus

Pray for:

- **God to fill you with the Holy Spirit.**
- **God to give you a deeper appreciation for the sacrifice Christ made for you on the cross and a clearer understanding of the blessings you have because of the cross.**
- **Those on your prayer list.**

Appendix A

Daily Prayer List

List five or more people whom you want the Lord to bring into His fold in preparation for Christ's soon return. These should be the people whom you plan to pray for and to reach out to during the next forty days. They should be people who have either left the church or who never were members of the church, and they should be people who live near enough to you so that you can invite them to church sometime during the next forty days.

1. _____   _____

2. _____   _____

3. _____   _____

4. _____   _____

5. _____   _____

Pray for these individuals every day, claiming the scriptures below on their behalf. (These are taken from *The Praying Church Sourcebook,* pp. 128, 129.)

- That God will draw them to Himself (John 6:44)
- That they seek to know God (Acts 17:27)
- That they believe the Word of God (1 Thessalonians 2:13)
- That Satan be bound from blinding them to the truth, and that his influence in their life be "cast down" (2 Corinthians 4:4; 10:4, 5)
- That the Holy Spirit work in them (John 16:8–13)
- That they turn from sin (Acts 3:19)
- That they believe in Christ as their Savior (John 1:12)
- That they obey Christ as Lord (Matthew 7:21)
- That they take root and grow in Christ (Colossians 2:6, 7)

Prayerfully use the "Activities to Show You Care" (see appendix B) list to determine what the Lord wants you to do to reach out to those on your prayer list during the next forty days.

Also, be sure to pray every day for the visitors' Sabbath and/or evangelistic meetings, if these activities are planned for the end of the forty-day program.

Appendix B

Activities to Show You Care

The following are suggestions of things you can do for those on your prayer list to show that you care for them. Add to this list as the Lord leads.

1. Call to say what you appreciate about them.
2. Mail a card sharing what God puts in your heart to tell them.
3. Send a piece of encouraging literature.
4. Call and pray with them.
5. Invite them to be guests in your home for a meal.
6. Give an invitation to go out to lunch with you.
7. Send them a birthday card when it's their birthday.
8. Send a card expressing encouragement.
9. Take them something you cooked.
10. Invite them to accompany you shopping, going to a museum, or something similar.
11. Send them a get well or sympathy card when appropriate.
12. Give their children birthday cards and gifts when appropriate.
13. Invite them to attend church with you.
14. At the appropriate time, ask whether they would like to receive Bible studies.
15. _____
16. _____
17. _____
18. _____
19. _____
20. _____

If a visitors' Sabbath or evangelistic meetings are planned at the end of the forty days, be sure to invite those on your prayer list to these events.

Appendix C

Suggested Greeting for Prayer Contact

Hello _____, (Interest's name)

This is _____. (Your name)

My church is having a special emphasis on prayer and is requesting that we choose five individuals for whom we are to pray during the next forty days. I have chosen you to be among the five for whom I will be praying. What would you like for me to pray for in your behalf? It could be for your family, for a job, for a health issue, and so on.

(Write down what they want you to pray for.)

_____

_____

_____

I appreciate the opportunity to pray especially for this for you during the next forty days.

Thanks _____, (Interest's name)

I'll keep in touch.

Appendix D

After the 40 Days of Prayer and Devotional Studies

Now that you have completed this forty days of prayer and devotional studies, you probably don't want the fellowship you are enjoying with the Lord to fade away. So, what should you do next? One possibility is that you begin studying in greater detail the subjects presented in this devotional. Many books in the Adventist Book Centers as well as books listed on my Web site, www.spiritbaptism.org, present these subjects. If this is your desire, I would suggest that you continue with your prayer partner and that you consider inviting others to join you, thus forming a study/prayer fellowship group. This will enable the Lord to strengthen the experience with Him you've been having during the past forty days. If you haven't studied the previously published 40 Days devotional books, I would suggest you begin studying one of them.

Second, continue to pray for those on your prayer list and to reach out to them. Also, add others to your list as the Lord leads, and as a group, plan activities to which you can invite those on your prayer lists to attend.

Christ wants personal daily devotional study, prayer, and reaching out to others to become an integral part of your life as a Christian. If these aspects of your life end when you complete the forty days of prayer and devotional study, you won't grow into the fullness of Christ that He desires you to experience. Also, it is through these spiritual practices that we prepare for Christ's return—for they are the only way our relationship with Christ develops and grows.

May the Lord abundantly bless your continued devotional study and prayer time with Him, and your efforts to share Him with others.

The Eternal Song
of the
Redeemed

In this life we can only begin to understand the wonderful theme of redemption. With our finite comprehension we may consider most earnestly the shame and the glory, the life and the death, the justice and the mercy, that meet in the cross; yet with the utmost stretch of our mental powers we fail to grasp its full significance. The length and the breadth, the depth and the height of redeeming love are but dimly comprehended. The plan of redemption will not be fully understood, even when the ransomed see as they are seen and know as they are known; but through the eternal ages new truth will continually unfold to the wondering and delighted mind. Though the griefs and pains and temptations of earth are ended and the cause removed, the people of God will ever have a distinct, intelligent knowledge of what their salvation has cost.

The cross of Christ will be the science and the song of the redeemed through all eternity. In Christ glorified they will behold Christ crucified. Never will it be forgotten that He whose power created and upheld the unnumbered worlds through the vast realms of space, the Beloved of God, the Majesty of heaven, He whom cherub and shining seraph delighted to adore—humbled Himself to uplift fallen man; that He bore the guilt and shame of sin, and the hiding of His Father's face, till the woes of a lost world broke His heart, and crushed out His life on Calvary's cross. That the Maker of all worlds, the Arbiter of all destinies, should lay aside His glory, and humiliate Himself from love to man, will ever excite the wonder and adoration of the universe. As the nations of the saved look upon their Redeemer, and behold the eternal glory of the Father shining in His countenance; as they behold His throne, which is from everlasting to everlasting, and know that His kingdom is to have no end, they break forth in rapturous song, "Worthy, worthy is the Lamb that was slain, and hath redeemed us to God by His own most precious blood!"

The mystery of the cross explains all other mysteries. In the light that streams from Calvary the attributes of God which had filled us with fear and awe appear beautiful and attractive. Mercy, tenderness, and parental love are seen to blend with holiness, justice, and power. While we behold the majesty of His throne, high and lifted up, we see His character in its gracious manifestations, and comprehend, as never before, the significance of that endearing title, "Our Father."

It will be seen that He who is infinite in wisdom could devise no plan for our salvation except the sacrifice of His Son. The compensation for this sacrifice is the joy of peopling the earth with ransomed beings, holy, happy, and immortal. The result of the Saviour's conflict with the powers of darkness is joy to the redeemed, redounding to the glory of God, throughout eternity. And such is the value of the soul that the Father is satisfied with the price paid; and Christ Himself, beholding the fruits of His great sacrifice, is satisfied.—Ellen G. White, *The Great Controversy*, pp. 651, 652.

Notes

Notes

Notes

Notes

Notes

Notes

Notes

Notes

Notes

Notes

Notes

Notes

Notes

Notes

Notes

Notes

Notes

Notes

Notes

Notes

Notes

Notes

Notes